WHILE LISTENING TO THE ENIGMA VARIATIONS

NEW AND SELECTED POEMS

DIANE FRANK

GLASS LYRE PRESS

Copyright © 2021 Diane Frank
Paperback ISBN: 978-1-941783-74-0

All rights reserved: Except for the purpose of quoting brief passages for review, no part of this book may be reproduced or transmitted in any form or by any means, electronic or mechanical, including photocopying, recording, or by any information storage and retrieval system, without permission in writing from the publisher.

Design & Layout: Steven Asmussen
Cover photograph: "Dawn at McClure's Beach"
  © Jeffrey S Bartfeld

Glass Lyre Press, LLC
P.O. Box 2693
Glenview, IL 60025
www.GlassLyrePress.com

While Listening to the Enigma Variations

New and Selected Poems

Acknowledgments

Deep appreciation to Ami Kaye of Glass Lyre Press for her vision, her poetry, and her desire to publish this book; to Steven Asmussen for his skill and art in book design.

Blessings to my mentors: Stephen Dunn, Robert Bly, Kathleen Fraser, and Daniel J. Langton. I've always had the gift of the right teacher at the right time. Blessings to Gary Snyder, who told me the story of the Princess who Married a Bear.

Special thanks to the musicians in the San Francisco Symphony, especially Jill Rachuy Brindel. Many of the poems in this book were inspired by your concerts. Special thanks to Urs Leonhardt Steiner and the musicians in the Golden Gate Symphony – I love playing music with you. Blessings to Matthew Arnerich, who composed the "Tree of Life Variations," inspired by my poem and performed by the Golden Gate Symphony.

Grateful acknowledgment to the following magazines and anthologies in which some of these poems were previously published: *Blue Unicorn, The Cimarron Review, Briar Cliff Review, Rattle, The MacGuffin, Pirene's Fountain, Poetry Breakfast, Haight Ashbury Literary Journal, Kumquat Meringue, Flash Boulevard, The Contemporary Review, Poetrybay, The Long Islander, Cloudbank, The Urbanite, Gallery Works, Antenna, Syracuse Poems, Sugar Mule, Night Roses, Miramar #5, Voices International, Museweek, Cyclamens and Swords, Vistas & Byways, The Homestead Review, Levure Littéraire, The Iowa Source, The Christian Science Monitor, PoetryMagazine.com, Redheaded Stepchild, Alchemy, Carquinez Poetry Review, Encore, Convergence, Worksheet, Maelstrom, The Cutting Edge, Conceit Magazine, nebu[lab], Albany Poetry Examiner, Majestic Isles Newsletter, Conch.es, sisterfrombelow.com,* and *Women's Voices for Change*. "Turtle Island" was published in translation by Tozan Alkan in Istanbul, Turkey.

Anthology publications: *Carrying the Branch: Poets in Search of Peace; Words In Concert: Poetry Inspired By Classical Music; Pirene's Fountain: Silk and Spice; Collateral Damage; Fire and Rain: Ecopoetry of California; Allegro & Adagio; Eternal Snow; Bear Flag Republic: Prose Poems and Poetics from California;*

Voices on the Landscape: Contemporary Iowa Poets; Leaves by Night, Flowers by Day; The Dryland Fish: An Anthology of Contemporary Iowa Poets; River of Earth and Sky: Poems for the Twenty-First Century; Magnum Opus: 360 Poems by 360 Poets from 60 Countries; AMORE: A Collection of Love Poems; Eclipsed Moon Coins: Twenty-Six Visionary Poets; Voices Israel; Fog and Light: San Francisco through the Eyes of the Poets who Live Here; Jewish Poems for the Third Millennium; In the Light of Peace; Suddenly the Earth is Singing; Long Island Sounds; Writing Outside the Lines; This Enduring Gift: A Flowering of Fairfield Poetry; The Art of Awe; and *Second Wind: Words and Art of Hope and Resilience.*

Multimedia: The Iowa Telepoem Booth.
Erik Ievins, Matthew Arnerich, Rebecca King, and Jan Pusina have composed music for my poems.

Praise for Diane Frank's Poetry

"Diane Frank's terrific *While Listening to the Enigma Variations: New and Selected Poems,* shows us a poet over a long and rich career who is undefeated by the acknowledged difficulties of living an affirmative life. She concludes an elegy to a friend by saying, 'Shine your light into the dark world,' and this is what Frank does in her poems. She's an ecstatic poet, who finds joy in music, dance, poetry, and, in general, in art itself. A book to have by your bedside when things seem bad."

Stephen Dunn,
Winner of the Pulitzer Prize

"Tomas Transtromer once said that his poems are meeting places for souls. In this world where one does not always feel entirely at home, it is with a sense of recognition that one enters a Diane Frank poem, with all its exotic quirks, and rather than feel it to be strange, feel it to be a habitable, companionable place of kindred spirits."

Thomas Centolella,
author of *Almost Human*

"In this new and startling collection, Diane Frank's poems transcend not just genres but entire dimensions. When she speaks to J.S. Bach, she really means it and when Bach speaks back, she listens – entirely – the way certain moths perceive sound via their whole body, even their wings. How is this accomplished? It will seem to come through the poems themselves – their music, tonal qualities and subjects, yet it goes even deeper as it pushes up like *duende* through the soles of your feet. The voice is declarative, emphatic, spirit driven. She will tell you, '*When a buffalo enters your dream, / listen for arpeggio hooves, / the weight of music, / a copper moon / above a vanishing prairie*' and you will, you must listen."

Lois P. Jones, author of *Night Ladder*
Radio Host, KPFK's Poets Café

"These poems of love returning to love, and light returning to light, are a heart gone supernova. Page by page Frank burns a path to her readers' hearts. The alignments are profound, the connections electric – from heart to bone, from marrow to star. These are radiant poems, where we earthbound creatures may find simultaneous escape and renewal."

George Wallace, Walt Whitman Birthplace Writer in Residence

"There may be those who think of poetry as optional, but Diane Frank's *While Listening to the Enigma Variations* does not support that thinking, since it addresses a hunger you didn't know you had, first with trace nutrients of the soul, and as you progress, with the solid food of organic experience. Read, savour and be nourished."

Paul Stokstad, author of *Butterfly Tattoo* and *Some Kind of Miracle*

"Diane Frank can enter, at will, that region where visions reveal themselves like snapshots. She transcribes these as jewel-like images on the page, through a vocabulary steeped in the natural world and the insistent predilections of the human heart."

Nancy Berg, author of *Oracles for Night-Blooming Eccentrics*

"Here is a book to treasure, to take down frequently for no particular reason, a book to help us remember why we took to poetry in the first place."

Daniel J. Langton, Professor Emeritus, San Francisco State University

Contents

While Listening to the Enigma Variations

The Genie	1
The Waterfall at Ein Gedi	2
While Listening to the Enigma Variations	4
Leap	9
Tree of Life	12
Omen	14
The Year of Opposites	15
Gopi	18
Abstract Mermaid	19
Mahler on Race Day	21
Chicken	25
Pheasant	26
The Sky away from Here	27
Venantius	29
Nightmare in New York	31
That Las Vegas Concert	33
Somewhere in Tibet or in my Mind	36
Kaddish for My Mother	37
Fire Storm	39
The Princess who Married a Bear	42
Turtle Island	44
Grandma's Quilt	46
The Green Dress	48
While Listening to the Sonata for Violin, Cello and Piano by Matthew Arnerich	50
What the Earth Whispered	52
Piano Lessons	54
My Face Became a Dream	55

Visions from Egyptian Dreams

To Isis	59
Dark Tide	60
First Dream	62
All Alone in the Orchestra	64
Keeping Still	66
Thornden Park	67
Melinda	69
Climbing the Scaffold	70
Afterimages	72
unsent letter	73

Between Two Languages

Dancing at Old Threshers'	77
Need One Ticket	79
Goats	81
Planting Flowers in the Intuitive Garden	83
Swimming Upstream	85
Postcards	86
Between Two Languages	89
White Butterfly	90

The All Night Yemenite Café

The Seduction of Bathsheba	95
Driving South to the Dead Sea	100
The All Night Yemenite Café	102
Better by Moonlight	105
Gifts	107
Photograph from Okinawa	109
Wild Orchids	112
How to Jumpstart a Dream	114

The Winter Life of Shooting Stars

Parachute	121
Angel of Eros	123
Gypsy Honeymoon	125
The Winter Life of Shooting Stars	126
Black and White Photograph	131
Beyond the Walls	134
Violins of Hope	136
In the Voices of the Birds	138
Waltz	140

Entering the Word Temple

My Mother's Daughter	145
Visions from the Right Hand of the Madonna	147
Venus of the Birds	150
Autumn in Iowa	153
Meridians	154
Virgins in the Uffizi	158
Entering the Word Temple	161
Ascending	166
Market Street Angel	168
Tennis Ballet	170
Finding You	174

Swan Light

Dancing in Paradise Café	177
By a Farmhouse in Corvallis	179
Ring of Fire	180
Pool	182
Redwoods in the Early Morning	183
Swan Dream	184
Iowa Omen	185
Circle of Stones	186
Dawn after the Art Walk	188
Stripes of Light on their Bodies	189
Meditation on the MUNI	190
Butterflies	192
Late August	194
Requiem	195
Coda to a Transformation	196

CANON FOR BEARS AND PONDEROSA PINES

Dreams of the Ecliptic	201
Margalit	202
Magnificat	204
Ultra-Body over the Mountain	206
Cello Lesson	208
Under a Copper Moon	210
Canon for Bears and Ponderosa Pines	211
Joy, like a Purple Balloon	214
Igneous	215
What your Cat did during your Vacation at the Grand Canyon	217
When You Fly	218
Earthquake, 5 A.M.	219
Jar with Dragons	220
Six Months in Arosa	222
Best Day Ever	224
About the Author	227

While Listening to the Enigma Variations

New Poems

The Genie

The dancing girl in the yellow silk pants
shimmered in my dream.
She was a flame that kept burning in the morning.
If I bring her to Aladdin,
I can gaze into her chocolate eyes
and lose myself in the maze of her footsteps.

Aladdin thinks I am his servant,
but every morning I weave a dream
into the world where he walks by the river.

I hold my prism in the river of sunlight,
each wave of color a possibility
to weave footsteps into the world
I paint every morning.
I can dream or disappear
into the longing for the light
that becomes invisible
inside the bronze of my lamp.

Every morning, you choose
to dance or disappear.

The Waterfall at Ein Gedi

She danced inside her memories
like an antelope
climbing the waterfall at Ein Gedi,
her face reflected in the water
then deconstructed
as it cascaded into the pool below.

The gypsies from King David's cave
tossed bones, their pattern
a victory in the stars
as they fell off the edge
of the horizon.

Later that night,
a moon behind the moon,
a kiss behind the kiss.
A meteor shower in bird shapes,
the birds flying to eternity,
flying to that moment
when the hummingbird alights
on your hand.

Five thousands years in the desert
a caravan to the oasis,
a goat, wild antelopes, strong shoulders.
A waterfall
breaking into the history of time.

Inside the caves,
the broken sound of water crashing
over rock,
the bones of our ancestors,
the secrets of the Dead Sea.

The Dome of the Rock,
the Western Wall
a landscape of stones
on a trail leading into the future.
Sweet honey in a Bedouin market,
a snake charmer, the cadence of an oud,
a call to prayer from the minaret.
A vision of peace inside the stones.

While Listening to the Enigma Variations

*Inspired by Elgar's Enigma Variations
performed by the San Francisco Symphony*

In a secret closet
under the house, a violin
weaves ethereal music – the melody
like enchanted wood you discover
by digging underneath
a cryptic message in a dream.
An enigma, a door
full of slanted light.

A braid of beeswax
melts into a candle, hand-dipped
into a river of monarch butterflies
while the world is waking up –
the first song
of a wood thrush,
a flute from high branches.

New rain in the forest,
a whisper of morning.
A meadowlark sings inside
the enchanted breath she blew
into a silver flute.
The girl she used to be
puts on her tutu
and dreams *en pointe*
on a pink silk ribbon.

The house was dark
except for one window
open to the summer moon.

A luna moth
flashed a mysterious pattern
on its wings.
Everyone inside the house
began to dream butterflies.

The sun reflects on brass –
French horn, oboe, flute,
a field of wild orchids
halfway up a mountain.
Strawberries, fingertips, her first kiss.
A meadowlark, an enigma.

A river swirled into a flood.
The bassoon became a willow,
branches reaching to rivulets of water.
An oboe echoed
the wet touch of the rain,
a seduction
into deeper water.

The memory of a swan,
but softly. The gathered swirls
of her green taffeta dress.
A green canoe paddling
in a light rain,
the lake filling with ripples.
A *pas de deux,* flashing of fireflies, a leaping –
the wide muscles of his legs
under the floating light
of a butterfly moon.

She dreamed in a minor key
every night by the river,

her cello a call to prayer
with the moon rippling the water
and then dreaming new worlds into being.
She wore her grandmother's necklace
with a moonstone and tiny rubies
into a sunrise somewhere else.

The cellist, bare feet
in a black tuxedo,
sending cryptic signals to the dragonflies
surrounded by eucalyptus trees.
Suddenly, a sunflower –
a fractal, a conch,
the enigma.
A kiss, a gentle sliding,
an oboe, an innuendo.

Her grandmother walks through memory.
Her garden, a river of marigolds –
petals full of sunlight.
In her farmhouse, sunflowers
leaning out of blue glass.
Through her window,
first light of the morning
soaring through a field of meadowlarks.

A dog jumps into the river,
the current pulling him
in an unexpected direction.
A ripple of light,
an island in the river,
the water singing over stones.
Marigolds in his fur,
doing the doggy paddle –
puppy love.

Memory is a minor chord,
a rivulet making its own path
down a mountain, water music
with silver waves in the sunlight,
rainbow trout swimming to spawn.
A cello echoing through the redwoods
where they hiked every Sunday
on another continent
across a wide ocean.

In those days,
love was always an enigma,
blueberries by the side of the trail,
an interrupted duet, the shadow of a dragonfly.
Wait! The sky is filling with music,
first light, a cello,
a cardinal weaving through branches
of eucalyptus.
In the distance, across an open field
the humming of bees,
a love that keeps singing.

Sunrise over the mountain,
all of the colors inside the light
felt but still hiding.
Suddenly, light is streaming
in leafy patterns across the walls,
down the path, across the rippling hills
to the Pacific. Once again
the world is blooming.

At the edge of the enigma
temple deer wander
through a forest of old growth trees,
alyssum, wild orchids –
light through branches, a sudden story
the whisper of
an almost forgotten language.
I tumble back through time.

Leap

For Victor Phillips

1.

He said, *If you dance your poems,*
you will feel them in your body.
You will become a bird,
an orbiting planet, a shooting star.
We were in a chapel
at a small university in Iowa,
his arms well trained in ballet.
What I most remember about that night
is when he said "Leap!"
and put me into a lift.
An amazing way to fly.

At that time in our lives
we were all searching
for elusive perfect forms –
in the sky garden of meditation,
the music of touch
and the joy of leaping.
We were reading Castaneda, the *Bhagavad Gita*,
Robert Bly, Mirabai, Rumi,
Yoga Vasistha –
tumbling in angst and joy.
I read about the green flash
in an Annie Dillard book,
then saw it for the first time
over the Temple by the Lake
at Pokhara, Nepal
after 24 days of trekking around Annapurna –
flying monkeys in every direction,
a vision from a Himalayan dream.

2.

You can see a light around him
as he sits on the stage of the San Francisco Ballet
before the performance of Don Quixote.
He's been training to do
this leap, this moment –
all of his life. He says to himself,
Basilio, don't worry, just dance.
Legs, are you still there?

In the wings, he gathers feathers,
then leaps onto the stage
loving the moment, having a great time.
He's laughing at windmills, and behind a curtain,
Sancho is ready to ride on a white donkey.
And Dulcinea . . .
You know she's looking at you,
even when her eyes seem to be somewhere else.

On the stage, you cannot hide anything.
The music takes you inside – now leap!
Nureyev whispers, *If I did it, you can do it.*
It's his choreography.
Beautiful but terrifying.
Basilio is ready to lift his partner with one hand.
Dulcinea, this is your moment –
Leap!

Classical ballet is so hard.
You fall, you get up, you try,
you leap through the ring of fire
until you do the impossible.
I think of my friend in the chapel,
that night of poetry, my first leap.

If it hadn't been for the AIDS epidemic,
he would still be dancing.

3.

Twenty years later, he is a hummingbird
streaking across my garden.
The green dance of early morning,
a glissando waterfall dip,
calla lilies stretching toward
light that has been traveling through time.
At the edge of the sunset,
a tidal shift, a green feather,
the sky field of aurora borealis,
rippled light.

Somewhere in a dream,
he steps out of a garden of strangers
into a whir of grasshoppers
and slides down the earth tunnel,
shivering and shimmering.
As he pulses through the birth canal,
full of prayers and promises,
undiscovered constellations
are looking at themselves
through his eyes.

Tree of Life

Kaddish for Dr. Jerry Rabinowitz

It's a form of praying,
to hold the darkness inside yourself
and embrace it
the way you would hold water
in a flowing river.

To wake up
with tears flowing from a dream
your face a field
of milkweed
as the pods scatter
in a wind of prayer
embracing the growing cold.

I remember where he sat
by the window
at the bottom of the flood plain
where the rivers emptied
into the streets that afternoon.
Fire trucks creating a wake
as they moved through the water.

And when the bullets came
he ran toward the shattering souls,
following his instincts
always to help,
to heal the wounded
and the dying.

His friends
hold each other
reaching out through time
and a dark river –
holding seeds planted long ago
by the Tree of Life,

say Kaddish in front of an open
Ark of the Covenant.

He would want you to find your light
and embrace it again,
to walk back into the forest
we call the world.

Hold his memory
the way you would hold his face.
Let his voice ripple
through time.
Where the trunk of a redwood tree
thick with the rings of centuries
was burned by lightning,
shine your light
into the dark world.

Omen

Through the scimitar shadows
by the 19th century church and graveyard,
the world is getting darker.
Crescents of light on the church walls,
slivers of hay still glowing
in a field of tiger lilies.

A morning sunset
over the ponderosa pines
and at the totality
a hush, applause, a dark feather
first light of the corona
around a dark sun.

The owl wakes up from its dream.
The Labrador quiet
at the feet of a young boy.
We traveled to this place
following a trail through time
in the footsteps of
ancient astronomers to view
a strange light.

And then that first ray of light
of the world beginning again.

The Year of Opposites

Everyone gets into the truck. Also the goat.
    We have hay for the goat,
        a watermelon to slice for everyone else.
Everyone is dancing barefoot in Tiberius,
    watching the tourists baptize one another
        in the Jordan River.
Everyone is hoping a bomb won't go off
    when they visit Jerusalem –
        by the Wall or in a café
            in toss distance from
                a palm-size stone or a molotov cocktail.

Those days I was working with the gardener
    who spoke fluent Hebrew, Arabic and English
        at Kibbutz Yachad in the Northern Galilee.
It was better than working in the kitchen,
    where the cook, who only spoke Hebrew,
        would point to a huge pile of cucumbers,
            and say, *Green. Wash.*
Or a stack of red peppers –
    Red. Wash.
        Or a sink full of pots.
            Wash.

I spoke Hebrew with a Palestinian taxi driver
    who didn't know English.
He called the place I asked him to drive me
    Sof Olam – end of the world.
Two weeks later, everyone in Jerusalem
    swarmed the streets on Independence Day.
My friends told me that if a bomb
    was going to explode,
        it would be tonight and here.

The bomb went off in our neighborhood
    at 2:00 in the morning.
My dreams for the rest of the night –
    a Picasso mosaic of fractured gardens,
        light being sucked out of everything.
In Sfat, a Kaballist rabbi read my palm.
    He told me about the future I would avoid
        by leaving.

In a dream, I saw myself –
    a young woman with a scar,
        a field of tiger lilies, an ocean of sky.
A house with a balcony, maybe split timber,
    maybe redwood or white oak
        that grew long ago in a forgotten forest.
White deer ran through the garden –
    their bodies almost made of light.

Two weeks later, in Amsterdam,
    they detained me in the basement of the airport,
        found my suitcase on the tarmac,
walked me to the plane,
    took the magazine I was carrying out of my hand,
        made confetti of my future,
            and sent me out of the war zone.

We didn't bend with the wind;
    we grew steel in our spines.
Every scar has an edge,
    a canyon, a crater of the moon.
In my house of dreams and split timber,
    I toss sunflower seeds in the garden,
        a shower of tiger lilies, oriental poppies.
I dig in my toes,
    and start to grow.

Life is a koan,
    and the most effective drum
        is the one that makes no sound.

Gopi

She is wrapped inside herself
    like the water inside the earthen pitcher
        she holds. Notice the way
she cradles the clay
    like the orbits of a planet or a baby.
        Krishna knows
she hears every note
    he is playing for her
        in her breast, her womb, her throat.
Her soft lips in the shape
    of the tune he plays.
        Notice the way the blue of her veil
wraps the gold of her sari
    and brushes against the blue
        of his shoulder,
wrapped in the silk of the Milky Way.
    They are lit by the moon
        through branches.
Yes, he knows the whole story –
    he is playing it through his flute,
        silver notes that arc through time,
weave through her hair,
    seduce her dreams and
        pull her into the future.

Abstract Mermaid

Inspired by a painting by Rosalind Brenner

As she crossed the bridge,
    she walked over time,
carrying a basket of pears
    in the early morning light.
Brushes and paint,
    the sun and the moon
        swirling out of expectations and form,
           orbits of color
                searching for a new shape.

    Earlier in her life
        art was a simple rendering –
a sunset, a willow branch, a melon
    a deer running across a field
        of sunset hay or wildflowers,
    but the shapes lost the ability
        to hold themselves.

    They became stars,
        meteors, a supernova of color
at the moment the star collapses.
    Light, shape and form
        like unexpected lovers
           curling around each other,
                finding a new shape every morning.

    It was a time in her life
        when shapes began to sing
and she could hear their interweaving melodies.
    Life was what she saw
        walking across fields of sunflowers
in a warm summer wind,
    roses by the side of the road
        every petal having its own dream.

    The petals filled the sky
        like meteor showers in August
arcing across midnight
    and the field where she walked in the moonlight
        at three o'clock in the morning
            tossing time through a prism of light.

    The world was what she saw
        and would never see again –
a painting of lovers in the early morning
    by the beach littered with tiny stones
        of agate, jade and jasper,
    the lovers searching for shape,
        an arm or a leg,
            a fish leaping out of the water

    And back into the thin ray
        of morning's first light,
the diffracted prism of time
        where everything shimmers.
She painted to carry these moments
    across the bridge of time.

Mahler on Race Day

*"I shall soar upwards:
To the light which no eye has penetrated!" – Gustav Mahler*

In concert black, we carry two cellos
to the N-Judah streetcar
on Bay to Breakers Sunday
to play Mahler's Second Symphony.
We take seats in the front of the train
next to a unicorn, a dragonfly,
runners in rainbow tutus,
and a caveman with a leopard Santa Claus Hat.

Erik's tuxedo, bow tie and hot pink cummerbund –
well, everybody's in costume.
We sit across from a furry gray cat
and an angel with a red, white and blue halo.

To my left, a couple holding hands
and wearing the medals they got
when they crossed the finish line.
She's dressed like a bumblebee,
fuzzy antennas waving from her headband.
He carries a bouquet of larger-than-life sunflowers.

More people board the streetcar –
a three-eyed alien, a troll with pink hair,
human-size mice and bunnies.
A leopard with a fanny pack
and a six pack.

A woman who flew in from Boston
tells me the Bay to Breakers is her 73rd birthday party.
We invite her to the Mahler concert.
She started piano lessons at age 66 –
no mother to tell her
the piano won't fit in her house.

A family of bumblebees climbs into the streetcar
with black antennas and black tutus.
One of them tells me the wings
helped her up the Hayes Street hill.
Standing in the aisle,
butterfly hats, butterfly wings, butterflies.

A cello isn't out of place in this crowd.
I invite a butterfly to the concert,
but she prefers early music.
I tell her we played Beethoven's Ninth Symphony last year.
"Beethoven? That's hardly early music!"

A bear in a fuzzy costume
says that Mahler is so much better
than the new music concert he heard last weekend –
sirens and pots and pans.
The rainbow caterpillar agrees.
"Mahler has melody, chord structure, immaculate timing
and thundering beauty."

Entering the streetcar –
metallic space cylinder.
Svelte runner in orange neon shorts
and rainbow snake earrings.

Bay to Breakers – 7.46 miles,
a marathon up and down San Francisco hills
from the Bay Bridge to the Pacific Ocean.
Mahler, quite a workout –
27 pages in the cello part.
Allegro maestoso at the starting gate.
My teacher's advice:
"At the downbeat, play as fast as you can.
Keep running!"

At Van Ness Station, exit the streetcar.
Up the stairs, down the street, cross the race at Hayes.
Traffic signals help, as we weave two cellos
between the tutus.

A few minutes before the call,
we find the side door to the Herbst Theatre
and a friend who plays French horn
for the San Francisco Ballet.
Bill says, "Mahler's Second Symphony
at the Herbst Theatre?
Good for you! But is the building
large enough to hold that piece?"

Curtain, conductor, start.
It's under my fingers,
and I keep intense focus as I play.
Waves of beauty and mystery.

The soprano soloist was one of the sent-down children
during the Cultural Revolution in China.
She sang to keep herself sane,
then emigrated across the Pacific to study opera.
The mezzo, a Southern Belle, with honey voice
and tango flowers in her hair,
would do herself honors at Mardi Gras.

It's a hauntingly beautiful and mystical piece,
from the opening run
to our standing ovation.
After the applause,
after "we really did this thing,"
in the aura of post-concert afterglow,
time to take cellos back to the Outer Sunset.

On the streetcar, we sit inside
a hive of bumblebees.
A butterfly takes our photograph –
tuxedo and concert black, holding cellos.
For the next week, Mahler,
a fat moon and rainbow tutus in my dreams.

Chicken

I was riding the N-Judah streetcar when an old Chinese woman got on with a chicken at Montgomery Street. As the door closed, the chicken jumped out of her bag and started squawking and running around the streetcar. She caught the chicken, stuffed it back into her bag. Everybody was watching, with a can-you-believe-this smile. Her feathers were pointed to the sky – the chicken was trying to fly and find her freedom. I came home feeling shaken by what I had seen, as I'm sure this story will not have a happy ending.

I wanted to let that beautiful bird fly, and at the same time, I knew I could not take away the old woman's food. Her face was creased like a river with muddy banks. Fish leaping out of the water. She got off at the same stop I did, and the chicken was sticking its head up out of the bag, looking for sky, a chick, or maybe a tree. Birds on the street were calling to her chicken. The Guardian Angel of Chickens was whispering, "Lay an egg. Maybe the old woman will change her mind."

The old woman was so pleased with herself. She had eyes from Guangdong, dreams of hot and sour soup, a sack of bok choy, and memories of hard times in China with no chicken. She was planning to feed her grandchildren a feast. A dream interfered. Sharks, swordfish, pirates, dark water. Now, everything reminds me of the chicken – what I think, what I eat, what I dream – so maybe that's why I'm telling you this story.

> Lost chicken escapes
> flies over rainbow
> follows a ray of sunlight
> over a field of golden corn
> does not become soup.

Pheasant

It was the most sensual meal I had ever eaten. Roadkill pheasant. "Joanne has a really good nose," Joya explained. "She can tell if the meat is fresh. Just a few minutes before we found it, the pheasant was still flying."

At the time, I was living in a small university town in Iowa – not always easy for someone from San Francisco. Joanne and Joya were people I could be myself with, and vice versa. They loved birds, and if they found a hawk, an eagle, or a pheasant dead by the side of the road, they'd pull over, honor the bird, pluck the feathers, and use them for a headdress or a ceremonial shield.

More food in that bird than two people could eat, so Joanne and Joya invited me to dinner before my evening class. They lit the table with candles and filled their rose-colored vintage glass plates with pheasant, stuffing, sweet potatoes, brussel sprouts and cranberry sauce. An early Thanksgiving. Everything smelled like the most delicious incense. Everything tasted like ambrosia. Before that night, I did not know that food could put you in an altered state of consciousness. It was really hard to leave that table when it was time to teach my evening class, even though it was poetry.

> Rainbow bird flies home.
> Blessed, filled with light, to open sky.
> Honor the feathers.

The Sky Away from Here

Somewhere, the moon turned copper.
Druids circled Stonehenge in amber robes.
My astronomy professor was on his balcony
with a telescope.
I was in San Francisco, under a thick cloud cover.

In the sky away from here,
shadows of buffalos ran across the moon
and coyotes howled their dirge to the dark night.

In London, a coven of moon-clad women
swept their homes, cooked moon soup,
chanted the old stories,
wore moonstones.

In the Zagros Mountains,
Sufis gathered in a stone circle,
read Rumi for an oracle,
became dervishes at midnight.

In Kyoto, a geisha in Pontocho
wore a kimono painted with a silk moon,
brushed her lover with a feather.

And in the Gatsby Land of the Long Island beaches,
two lovers bathed in a tide pool
using the dark of the moon
as a cover.

In San Francisco, I entered my dreams
as the rain pounded disappointment on my window,
but in the sky away from here,
luminous tattoos
danced across the sky
and shattered into new constellations –

the buffalo, the geisha,
the feather,
a tide pool of lovers
on the far side of the moon.

Venantius

He was the crazy man
singing the blues between cars
on the A Train –
levitating to the moon
on a painted trail of light.

At the Ringling Brothers Barnum & Bailey Circus,
he released the baby alligators from their cages
during the high wire act,
with lions jumping through feathered hoops
below. Around him, women riding horses
wore pink feathered plumes.
Hawkers sold cotton candy and crackerjacks.

He asked for a photograph
of me playing the cello,
my arm drawing the bow into a long, low note.
I was wearing silk, concert black,
my fingers breathing the music
I played that night.

Around my cello, he drew images
of bears, rivers, waterfalls.
Himalayan peaks,
where elephants, butterflies, fractals
dream in swirling colors
on a mountain trail.

He painted sacred syllables
in Sanskrit, Hebrew, Tibetan
and an ancient Kanji calligraphy –
what he heard inside the music.

After weeks of painting,
he tiptoed over the border

where his *amigos* from Mexico
put his painting in a mailing tube
and sent it to San Francisco.

Inside his meditation, a sanctuary
where the colors swirl and blend.
Outside his window, a river of humanity.
New York City is always a circus.

Nightmare in New York

While playing a 20th Century symphony

Everything happens in a taxi
driving down 42nd Street,
careening through time.
You can hear horns blaring in the distance.
In the back seat, the murderer
is watching *Psycho* on his cell phone.
The seats are bright red.

The music slows with the traffic,
now crawling down West 14th Street.
A ghost. A memory. A dream.
The Purple Onion. Green Tangerine.

Segue to back seat of taxi,
a black and white checkered cab.
His wet dream fantasy
is playing an oboe, or maybe an accordion.
The music is wearing fishnet stockings
and a black velvet cape.
The barista pulls out her whip.

Time shift – time warp.
It's 1955. Air raid drill.
Everyone is hiding under their coats
except for the class clown
tossing spitballs.

Viola accelerando.
The tempo is a wild card.
Raid at the Speakeasy.

The cyclotron
travels back in time.
Ritardando.
I desperately want to stop
Hiroshima.

Meno Mosso.
Affettuoso = 48. Emotion? Tenderness?
Slow. Waterfall of gardenias. Slower.

Segue to dinosaur bones
at the Museum of Natural History.
After the applause,
the bones begin to speak.

That Las Vegas Concert
For Naia

What is the velocity of a bullet?
The trajectory of lives
at a concert for young fans
of country rock stars?
And if that old man wanted to leave this world,
why did he have to take
a trainload of children with him?

She ran to the stage and hid in the packing case
of a concert speaker
to escape the barrage of bullets.
Someone told her to run,
thought the shooter was headed for the stage,
but the information was wrong.
It turned her into a fish in a barrel,
an ant under a foot,
a girl with three bullets in her arm.

What is the velocity of light?
In a rocket, it looks like the speed of light.
An observer can be surprised
by formulas and calculations they don't understand.
Keep running. Keep running.

An off duty fireman
took off his belt to make a tourniquet
and kept her from bleeding out.
As she started to fall asleep,
he tapped on her chest and said,
Stay with me.
You're not going to die today.

Shine a flashlight into the world,
into the dark night.

Breathe into the humming,
where the sun has become empty,
dreaming of rocks, planets, a young girl.

Time freezes and life
starts rushing back.
The fireman lifts her over a wall,
into a car, to the hospital.
Triage surgery,
three bullets removed from her arm.

Information is coming from too many directions.
Time becomes longer. Clocks are slower
between world lines.
Prayer for black holes
swallowing rifles in spacetime.

Now, mysterious music carrying
the voice of a thousand prayers,
calling her back to the world again.

Ignore everything you've heard
about observers affecting reality.
Bullets. Electromagnetism. The speed of light.
The force lines of shrapnel
reshaping her hand.
And what does this do to my world
where it isn't safe to listen to music?

Ten weeks later,
a young woman walks back
into the classroom where she teaches young children –
her arm in a cast,
her bones held together by titanium.
Her students stand up and cheer.

She doesn't tell them about the alarm on her door,
or how many months of physical therapy she will need
before she can use her arm again.
She doesn't tell them what she dreams at night.

If I step outside of the world,
I can see the curve of the planet.
You have to step outside of things
to measure them.
Her smile. The smile of time.

Life is a fortune cookie,
a flashlight shining into the emptiness,
gravitational waves from black holes,
a rocket careening
close to the speed of light.

The task ahead –
to stitch time back together.

Somewhere in Tibet or in my Mind

Late at night, I think about atoms and stars,
layers of infinity
reaching out to the far expanse of the universe
where there is no edge,
reaching in to the core of atoms
layer after layer
of particles, energy, light.
There is something even beyond this
which I can feel
but don't completely understand.
Somewhere, on a mountain
in India or Tibet,
a monk is chanting *sutras* and carving *mani* stones.
He sees what I see
as a Goddess with a Thousand Arms,
and the mountain whispers her name.

Kaddish for My Mother

You need to play this music
the way the colors blur and intensify at sunset.
Wrap your legs around the wood
and lean into the sound.

This piece demands
that you reach into a deeper part of yourself
and access more power.
It makes you climb higher on the fingerboard
and learn how to do it musically.

Saying an ancient prayer in Aramaic
does not give you the emotions
you feel from these strings.
Tears in the vibrato.
The voice of a tenor cantor.

You never did this before?
Now, climb the ladder of these notes.
Listen and make your fingers wail
the vibrato this piece requires.

And suddenly,
ancient cities are revealed to you.
Your mother's voice, the emotions.
She could inspire a room full of worshipers
to feel music inside a prayer –
indigo threads inside the weaving
of a prayer shawl.

The wood from the Black Forest
whispers its secrets.
Priestesses who knew the mysteries
are chanting from your strings.

When you were a girl, your mother
sang to you every night, two lullabies,
her voice rocking like a cradle in the trees.
Lean into your cello now,
with your arms, your heart, your knees –
the echo of her voice.

Fire Storm

For Sharon, who lost her home in the Calistoga Fire

1.

To watch her dance
at the end of the world,
her house surrounded
by flames of leaves,
the wind rearranging their patterns.

A broken compass
A book with the secrets of her face
A meeting with no one
An appointment to go nowhere
A deck of cards, a raw deal
A fire storm moving up her street.

When she wanted to go back home,
the house was gone.

2.

The night of the fire storm
she baked a sweet potato pie for dinner,
gathered a salad with wild arugula
and tomatoes from the garden,
a fiery red, a late bloom.

They were sleeping at his house that night
when, at 2:00 in the morning,
he heard his neighbors outside,
a crackling, a roar,
flames at the end of the street.

They ran to the car in their pajamas,
thinking they'd finish their dreams at her house
but the road was closed.
A few hours later,
they knocked on the door of a friend
in Petaluma,
where they stayed for the next two weeks.

3.

She crossed a bridge of bones
as fireworks deconstructed the sky.
She was gazing through a telescope,
searching for the black hole
at the center of our galaxy.

All of her questions deflected
against meteors scorching time
on their elliptical orbits.

Born on a wounded planet,
a team of astronomers
was searching for a new solar system
with carbon and water molecules,
the pool of life.

But they had to dream it first –
the language preceding the hologram
of the form and then creating it
with a whisper.

4.

The voice of the fire ripples through time
to a hidden dimension.
Always another fire in what could be Paradise.
In Brazil, soybean farmers set fire
to the Amazon Rain Forest.
They are burning the dreams of their grandchildren.
They have forgotten the Earth is a Goddess.
They have forgotten that humans need air.

We are praying to the Guardian Angels of the Earth,
but we don't know how to reverse time
or reverse the spin
of the lifespan of our planet.

The Princess who Married a Bear

A bear crawls into her room
    in the darkness.
The woman he embraces
        lights a candle to see
    the fur on his back,
        a city of dreams.

Listening to the Prelude
    of the Second Bach Cello Suite,
        she hears a forest of possibilities
    in the phrasing of every cadence –
the glowing of ancient trees
    and inside the vibrato,
        the hum of the earth.

It's the kind of beauty
    that makes her want
        the earth to endure.

What good fortune
    to have music in her hands,
        playing chords that have endured for centuries.
    What good fortune to marry the bear
        just before winter's hibernation.

During the long sleep of winter,
    she travels with dream bears,
        lumbering through dreamwood
            in an old growth forest.
By a fire below winter constellations,
        her Inuit grandmother sings to a snowy owl.
Her visions whisper a new season,
        peonies scenting a warm wind.

Night is always a mystery –
    the scent of a bear
        reaching through the darkness.
She plays it on the cello,
        her music embracing
    the heart, the trees, the earth.
She dreams the music of the mountain
    slow touching her skin.

Turtle Island

What if the world
    was created by a giant turtle
        swimming across the sky
            at the beginning of time?

What if the turtle
    carried dreams in her belly,
        giving birth to fish and stars?

What if the high flying tern
    marked the world lines of space and time
        with nets of aurora borealis?

What if the donkey said
    the humans are a joke, spinning through space
        juggling fire and ice?

What if the crab said
    crawl sideways if you want to uncover
        the dreams that are painted inside of shells?

What if the moon said
    the night will tell you secrets
        if you listen to the music inside of stones?

What if the shark said
    you will discover fish that glow like lanterns
        in deeper currents of ocean water.

What if the octopus said
    your dreams are tentacles
        into a future filled with fish and golden apples.

What if the turtle
    keeps swimming out of the sky
        to a universe hidden somewhere else?

What if the buffalos
    stampede with their ancestors across the Great Plains
        under an ocean of sky?

Buffalo Woman says
    the world is a dream or nightmare.
        Weave your visions with tender hands.

Grandma's Quilt

Fabrics from an earlier century,
these are the clothes she wore –
plaids, gingham, calico
hand-stitched into aprons
dresses and blouses with pearl buttons,
hand-knit socks in matching colors.

After she leaves this world,
her daughter patches the fabric
into a Grandma Quilt –
an 8-pointed star, stripes and triangles
arranged in a spiral
inside layers of color, her universe.
It was her way of managing grief.

Tea steaming in a copper kettle.
A house of Persian carpets
distributed among her five children
and their children.
Lenox china and silver
blessing a wedding she did not live to see.

With the fabric that remains,
her daughter designs a series of smaller quilts
for five siblings, eight grandchildren,
and two more for the next generation.
Suspended with cord and bamboo
from thirteen walls.
Another quilt for Grandpa,
who will grow sunflowers in his garden
with hundreds of species of rare, exotic plants
for three more years.

Above a moonlit cloud
with a silver lining
like the velvet in her antique dresser,
Grandma whispers in her silver voice.
Her daughter hears it in a dream
she doesn't remember in the morning,
but the cardinal singing by her window
brings memories of her mother
in a way she can't explain.

The world is full of color.
A ribbon of lines, a river of stars,
the brilliant yellow of a sunflower.
The music in every color is calling your name,
weaving memories of her voice
into the fabric of the blooming earth.
And from another world,
your mother invites you to weave
a river of light,
the gift of every new morning.

The Green Dress

For Bur McAllister

*"You come from some other forest
do you / little horse . . ." – W.S. Merwin*

You were too much of a leprechaun
to want to get old.
That night, in a dream
I took you to the San Francisco Symphony
and you choreographed Beethoven's Ninth.
The purists complained
and hardly noticed you were dancing barefoot,
your orange sneakers hanging on a tree
outside the window.

I was wearing that green sateen party dress
you gave me –
the one your mother sewed to dance in
when she was a younger woman.
After the Ode to Joy
we got up on the stage to waltz.
You were smiling that mischievous smile
you always wore,
hoping to lead me in a dance that would unfold
with unexpected turns and whirls
like the wind, weaving through filtered light
in a redwood forest –
something worthy of that green dress.

That was before you slid home.

A crowd of dancers gathered in the concert hall,
where the old poet you loved
asked us to dance the Little Horse.
Gracefully, with feeling.
I had the whole poem memorized
and recited it with my eyes closed.

As you walked off the stage,
out of the room,
you asked us to let the door close gently
as you followed the path back into the forest.

While Listening to the Sonata for Violin, Cello and Piano by Matthew Arnerich

Allegro Maestoso

> Dark and complicated.
> Hoola hoops in multiple directions,
> twirling simultaneously.
> Imagine three superballs let loose inside a pinball game
> made by M.C. Escher.
> Midnight in a rain forest,
> crosscurrents of exotic tropical birds
> below a waterfall.

Tempo di Valse

> Chopin meets Rachmaninoff
> under a tangle of vines in a rain forest.
> The tour guide keeps calling them back;
> it's like asking children to please stay on the trail.
> But off they go again, following dragonflies,
> blue notes in their wings.

Theme: Adagio

> Lullabye for his daughter
> swimming in the universe of the womb,
> about to be born.
> Listen to the way the stars are singing to her,
> and the way the notes echo
> inside the swollen pear of her mother's body.
> Two heartbeats weave harmonies
> through the amniotic sky.
> The world is illuminated with aurora borealis,
> and the last cello note is divine,
> spinning colors into the River of Birth.

Allegro Giocoso

    Now it all comes together:
    the Escher pinball machine becomes a video game,
    with Chopin and Rachmaninoff running around inside
    hurling snowballs at each other.

    Where the silver balls stop and resonate,
    tropical birds pause on branches
    and begin to sing –
    a crazy, exciting cacophony of sound.

    In the sky, a universe of stars,
    points of light in the vastness.
    Everything flying, dreaming, dancing.
    Behind the stage,
    an angel, a muse, a dragonfly
    laughing at the cosmic joke,
    loving it and blessing it.
    It's raining stars, the atoms of life,
    and new universes are being born.

    The baby is pushing down the birth canal
    as a family of migrant workers
    is planting olive trees
    that will be twisted and gnarled in a hundred years,
    still bearing fruit.
    The path weaves through the arbor,
    then opens to fields of lupine and lavender.
    In the distance, a round window
    below rafters of a farmhouse,
    the first cry of the newborn
    woven with the music of the sky.

What the Earth Whispered

Hanging from a silver chain
    The tooth of a yeti
    The tooth of a dream
The flame of a candle
    The flame of the stars
    The voice of infinite night
The moon in a corner
    The sky of a thought
    The words of a promise
Crashing into a red rock canyon
    The minotaur and the dinosaur
    After too many wars
Crop circles in a wheat field
    Pranksters, Druids or aliens?
    A ritual in blue flame
The crash of a civilization
    Just a few years
    After forgetting its dreams.

After forgetting its dreams
    Just a few years
    The crash of a civilization
A ritual in blue flame
    Pranksters, Druids or aliens?
    Crop circles in a wheat field
After too many wars
    The minotaur and the dinosaur
    Crashing into a red rock canyon
The words of a promise
    The sky of a thought
    The moon in a corner
The voice of infinite night
    The flame of the stars
    The flame of a candle
The tooth of a dream
    The tooth of a yeti
    Hanging from a silver chain.

Piano Lessons

Every afternoon, she plays the piano
      for an hour, metronome ticking
   with the screen door open.
      Outside, the neighborhood kids
play kickball in the street.
    She sees them running
      over her right shoulder.

It is two hours before dark,
    before the Moonlight Sonata –
      Beethoven's deaf fantasy
streaming through his window.
    The same light
      that shines through the starry leaves
        of the maple
brushing against the fence
      of her dreams.

Years later, the moon
      melts through her hands,
   music from who knows where –
      maybe sky, maybe ocean.
On the dance floor
      a stripe of moonlight
        shivering up her spine,
the night through starry leaves
      of her history.

My Face Became a Dream

My face became a dream,
and it went somewhere I don't completely understand.
The artist saw it from that angle
and could not explain it to me.
The dream was about music
I could feel but not play
until I left this world
and came back in another form.

The dream became a butterfly,
a prism refracting rainbows into another dimension,
a sonata flying through mysterious music.
It orbited a planet in another galaxy
and returned as the aurora borealis.

At 4:00 in the morning
an owl calls to the moon
through a sky full of fog.
Crickets hesitate.
At the edge of a dream,
just when I think I have nothing left to say,
the light starts shining.

Visions from Egyptian Dreams

and early poems

To Isis

*Isis is the Egyptian Goddess
of love, healing and resurrection.*

You appear in my room at 4 a.m.
You have just floated through the wall.
It must have been the desire of my tongue
for the smooth line of your collarbone.

There are photographs in the water,
Waves to dive under.
I try to keep my memories
dry.

But what is this music?
A flute.   Primitive   stone houses on the hill.
Leaves.   Cherry blossoms of light.
Warm mist after music.

It was only desire   music of arms.
Flute of tongue on the back of my neck.
Earth music of the iris
to plant again.

Dark Tide

For Tom and Katrina

It must be the music of the mind,
the way the mind switches
from one theme to another,
each new thought
like a shell
washed up by the tide,
leopard spots and curve examined
then washed back.

Your music is a dark tide,
in the chapel
your right hand silver
bells against the minor
of the left
droning in the sand.

Certain movies have this mood.
Ursula, in the caravan
of the gypsy
as table and children
disappear
like the silk dress
he is pulling off her shoulders.
The flood,
its haunting music
and her grandmother
with her China clocks
under the water.
The go-between
running his messages
through the heath
in quiet outrage.

In the chapel,
a Steinway, your jazz.
The chapel as moody
as a night at the ocean,
clouds in patchwork
over an echo of the moon.

Stars fly
above the crashing
with the speed and surprise
of your notes.
The moon appears,
then so dark
you can't see
the tide.

Your love is quiet.
Her music is hidden
like the bones of buffalos in Montana,
a dream of an open field,
tribal feathers of her ancestors.
Her toes uncover
a sand dollar at the beach.
Her Australian Shepherd, named Malo,
runs into the crashing waves,
circles back, runs into
a flock of pelicans.
They scatter and rise –
you don't know where
they are flying.
As she gathers the long fur
of her Shepard
into her olive arms,
her eyes are a dark tide.

First Dream

There's a deep, dark hole
in the open space
where the bathroom's supposed to be.
You could fall down there
to the coal lady.

My crib is made of iron
black as the world around my tiny eyes
round and open.
Below the crib are two orange lights
the kind that signal
while you wait for the train.

Listen, the train could be coming!
Down from the stars
and straight into the blackness
where I am waiting.
It could come and take me . . .

Back to what I knew
before I milli-inched my way
down the long corridor.
Back to the space
where I couldn't distinguish my mother
from a tree.

I crawl over the wrought iron,
inch my way down the ramp
slowly beyond the dark space
where you could fall down
to the coal lady.

My father
is in the living room
with two of his friends from college.

I remember the college –
he took me there on his shoulders.
He doesn't really notice me
as I crawl up on his lap –
safe from the orange fire
of the coal lady,
far away from the darkness
and the train.

All Alone in the Orchestra

A small audience is gathered in the church.
A collection of musicians on the altar,
playing Mozart,
the velvet and the pulpit pushed aside.
I play on the second stand in the cello section,
the last molecule in the comet's tail.
Does anyone understand the way I fly inside the music?
Surrounded by stained glass windows,
embracing the wood of old growth forests
in concert black and lace.

I put away my mind's telescope
and attempt to focus my attention.
I sway to follow these long notes
and try to go where they will take me.
I feel the movement in my back, my arms, my toes.
Then the comet in me flies off again.
Would anyone like to come along with me?
A cellist or the oboe player?
Hey you, playing over there,
I offer you –
my secret constellations,
the shadows in my corners,
the ivy growing all around my mind.

I can see you playing every instrument –
bass, cello, viola, violin . . .
Your body changes to fit each one.
French horn, bassoon, oboe, flute . . .
Your bones mold into every new position.
Now I see you play a clarinet.
Your spine is made of sparks,
around it
the rhythm of frantic moths
black and bound together by the night.

I see you turn into an owl,
                            a raven,
                                            the sky.

I feel the tempo of all your small animals.

My hand climbs the fingerboard –
allegro, crescendo,
the echo of Mozart's starling in the flute.
I'm bound by his essential gravity;
I orbit in his space.
I haven't missed a thirty-second note.
I lean into these notes; I sway;
I follow where they want to take me.

Suddenly, I'm not playing anymore.
I want to fly through the wings
of one of these angels of church-stained glass.
I could sing a note so high and pure
that all of you would break,
as I sit here quiet in my black and lace –
my arms embracing their angular space,
my fingers reaching, reaching . . .

And then, I'm far away from here.
It's snowing
and absolutely still inside.
My head is an open cage,
an amphitheater
with skeletons of the winter trees.
Silent birds fly out of my skull
like a high note on the cello
after the bow stops.

Keeping Still

I dreamed
we were helping each other
up a long mountain.
The mountain was made of words
and the moon
had a green shadow.

How would it feel
to hold you all night?
There's an earthquake
in my spine.

Thornden Park

In memory, everything is green –
aurora glowing in the sky over a mountain.
Green light filling a room,
tropical leaves in the greenhouse.
Green love, a green hill,
sliding with friends on cafeteria trays
down a path of snow.
We were green in our knowledge of the world,
on our backs, in the amphitheater
under a sky show of stars.

Through a telescope from an attic window,
my first view of the rings of Saturn.
In a blizzard during a snow storm,
my first ride in a snow mover with giant wheels.
In the stacks of the University library,
I was always searching for poets with women's names –
Diane Di Prima, Adrienne Rich, Denise Levertov.

In the house on the other side of Thornden Park,
he dreamed of intricate, interweaving harmonies;
I dreamed about my father.
Music and moonlight through a stained glass window.
Later, I watched an artist friend
sew legs on the bottom of a painting of two women
when she ran out of canvas.
The women leaned into the colors
the sky turns before the light disappears.

Everything on an impulse –
jump into the green VW bug,
drive to Niagara Falls at night
to see the moonbow on tumbling water –
a shimmering silver-white arc.

In April, drive to Key West
during spring vacation,
sleep on the beach
with the salty blue ocean crashing
into our dreams.

Everyone too absorbed in self discovery
to understand the ocean of tears
that fell out of what they touched
and let go of.
Climbing ladders and scaffolds
of buildings under construction.
We were under construction.
Yes, our lives were like that –
green in those days.

Melinda

five minutes past midnight
night before the full moon

she finishes
stitching purple yarn
through an old grey hat

he has been watching

the wax is dull yellow
flames flash on the Persian rug

his body assumes
the rhythm
of a Pinter play

in a mirror
she takes the form
of the highest
strains of Shostakovich

he looks into her eyes
only to see
the snow of earlier winters

Climbing the Scaffold

She left her violin
by the side of the music building
in its case – black around soft blue velvet
and climbed the scaffold
all the way to the highest
shaky board
with a cold wind riffling her hair.
Buildings on campus were always under construction
in those days. We liked to climb them
late at night.

Don't jump!
Your future is waiting.
You will hitchhike across Europe
and meet new friends. After medical school,
you will give birth to four children.
Don't jump!
That cellist who led you
up to his room late at night
isn't worth jumping off the roof.

We watched him play Boccherini
surrounded by stained glass on campus
and bluegrass cello on weekends
with the Down City Ramblers.
He was the embodiment of experiment,
and you never knew
who he was going to be on Monday.

The wind is speaking to you,
holding your dreams like the butterfly
you will become. Spread those colorful
wings inside your music,
not the sky, not this moment

where the music of the earth
is asking you to return.

Later, you will tell me
that you didn't climb high enough,
but the small hands of your children
reached through time
to your back, your legs, your feet
and brought you back home.

Afterimages

How do I know
if you see green
the way I do?

You talked last night
about ripples
on the cornea –

afterimages,
shadows
around the object.

A musicologist told me
that so-many cycles per second
equals E-flat.

But how does that sound
inside your ear?

And when I touch you,
do you see
the blue light
around my heart?

UNSENT LETTER

on a box of jasmine tea
i send you a wish
of tupelo honey

the song
of a yellow bird
through broken light

crumpled flowers and leaves
from a secret meeting
we never had

Between Two Languages

Dancing at Old Threshers'

Tangerine sunset floats low on the horizon.
The moon is orbiting around your hat.

I dance with you between rows
of early September corn,
your Amish beard a field of uncut hay.

I haven't memorized the map
of the constellations, but your eyes
are burning. The landscape of your muscles
ripples under your white muslin shirt.

You turn me two hands round
as the Great Bear rises in the sky
above your left shoulder.

There's a secret beneath my gingham apron,
a shower of falling stars
as we dance around the fire
kicking up the ground made hard
by late summer rain.

We orbit around the shapes
of our forefathers' stories –
a galaxy of seasons changing,
the stars a blur,
wood smoke and wisdom whirling.

As we circle around each other,
the bear wakes up from his dreaming,
hears the tinny music
of hammered dulcimer floating south.

He pulls corn out of the husks
and you open your mouth.

The moon cracks like a pumpkin.

The sparks brush your skin
like a woman with turquoise beads,
tan muscular arms
and the secrets of your shoulders.

I am the goose shadow dreaming
of the day the universe began,
singing the music of the next creation.

Need One Ticket

Mickey never bought tickets to the symphony. It was against her religion. We were San Francisco Symphony buddies in those days. After she stashed her car somewhere on Franklin Street – always easy with the help of Gladys, the Parking Goddess – we'd walk to Davies Symphony Hall and she'd hand me a small sign – Need One Ticket. The tickets always came, always offered by someone other than the beak-nosed hawker. Often free, and never for more than the few dollars we had in pocket. I didn't have a lot of money in those days.

We had side terrace seats for Pinchas Zuckerman playing Tchaikovsky's Violin Concerto, first tier for the New York Philharmonic, with a return the next night for Shostakovich. I would always be ready for her "let's go!" phone call. Hightail to the house she filled with art from the countries where she traveled. Hop into her Subaru and drive. On Monday nights, we were trail buddies for Israeli folk dancing, often with a tossed together meal. I can still see her in her kitchen with hand-rolled pasta, tomatoes from the Farmer's Market, fresh mozzarella cheese.

Mickey spent her teenage years in a detention camp in Dutch Indonesia during the Second World War. The Japanese were holding the Jews in case the Germans decided to deport them. She told me she worked as a carpenter and was able to survive with the extra helping of rice they gave her. She slept on a wooden bench and, somehow on the miracle train, escaped the terrible diseases that captured many of her friends. Years later she let me know how many coffins she hammered together. And who else would say these were some of the best years of her life because of the courage and love she felt in the community of women there?
Who else?

Tiny woman. Exuberant soul.
Dancing through life like a batik butterfly,
speaking at least twelve languages
delighting her dancer friends and strangers
with her passion for living.

Traveling around the world,
to swim the bluest lake,
to climb the highest mountain,
to find the weaver who could create
kilim that became magic carpets –

a carpet of flying colors
always ready for the next miracle.

Goats

We are walking on trails on Mt. Tamalpais. We come to a river by a wooden bridge, and he wants to kiss me. We are on a Persian rug by a fire, and he wants to hold me. He begins to learn how.

I am sleeping with him in a loft apartment. Actually, he is sleeping and I am awake. The loft is a dance studio on the second floor of a huge building. Mirrors on the wall. All of my furniture is in the southeast corner – my Japanese folding bed, the rattan chair, and a gardenia.

We are swimming in a lake on top of a mountain. Glaciers left flat stones close to the shore, and we lie beside them. His arms look exotic in the water. The lake ripples over his muscles, while the sun condenses tiny drops of water. The stones remind me of the lake where I met him. They remind me of the Dead Sea.

He says, "I love you, but part of me doesn't love you. We're going to be together for several months, but by August we will separate." He is thinking about our picnic – a loaf of sourdough bread, goat cheese, and tomatoes. I am thinking about the goats by the farmhouse yesterday. I wonder if he will leave me. I pause a bit to feel if it's true. Then I say, "No, I'm going to be the one to break off with you. You always make me do all the work."

We are back in the loft trying to sleep. He is on the bed, and I walk to the door. The dimensions of the room begin to distort. Now the door is on the wrong side and won't close completely. It's 2:30 in the morning. The door to the loft of the jazz musicians is open; it's their time of night. The light shines with their music. The music is edgy, staccato, and my door won't close completely.

I go back and lie on the couch by the gardenia. I want to be close to him, but he climbs the stairs. Now he is far away, on the other side of the goats. The room is invaded by thieves and demons – the kind that can get inside you. I tell them they have no power, but they say it isn't true. They are like incessant speech. Everyone I have known is far away – even the gardenia. I call out to the goats, and they come running through the walls.

Planting Flowers in the Intuitive Garden

I didn't plan where to put the irises.
The bulbs went in like a snowfall,
and two seasons later, when squawking geese
flew south across the moon,
poppy seeds scattered where they fell.

As the tangled roots of warmer weather
push their way to the deeper earth,
daffodils collide with tulips.
Blueberries twist their branches
around rose petals
like a dancer who has stretched so far
beyond her natural shape
that the form has to break.
I dance in the garden at night
with pink lace climbing my ankles
and my toes bruised like blueberries.

Every day I add another flower –
columbines surprising the lattices on the porch,
shasta daisies with double rows of petals
wild as ostrich feathers,
nasturtiums with edible blossoms.
Summer comes in a flood, but the wind is still breathing
with dahlias curling their leaves
toward unknown colors.

I want to dance at midnight in my garden,
with peonies bent to the ground
by thunderstorms.
I want to dream in a gallery of angels
surrounded by wildflowers
and a pasture of goats and sleep.

Every day I add another flower,
like the petaled surprise of love.
Every day the magenta blood of wild berries
stains my fingers and my cheeks.

Swimming Upstream

The angel only comes
when you need her.
She folds her wings over your eyes
to take away the pain.

You say that I was blind in a past life,
my fingers learned to see there.
They touch your edges like sculpture,
bring you beyond the dark spaces
to the river, swimming upstream
in holy water.

I dance to connect myself
with sun wheels
dream circles
human hands.

We walk with bare feet back
to the desert –
a shaman
in a circle of feathers
below an adobe sun.

When the Goddess came
her moonlight
was almost blinding –
Phoenix feathers
and flowers on her face,
feet of adobe.

I bring you gifts of adobe
and touch you with
fingers that learned to see
in a darker time.

POSTCARDS

1.
Three years ago you wrote and told me
there is an ongoing battle
between the dwarf and the human being
inside you. When we are together,
you say, "I know you."
It opens me. I break
into my gazelle body.
Every time, I let you inside me,
but I don't know why.

2.
We lie on the rocks in Africa.
Dreams float through the window.
Outside, birds collect on the telephone wires.
You know every melody.
You can separate each song
and call them by name.
In the dream you are climbing the silo.
You throw me a rope ladder
and pull me up with your strong Norwegian arms.
We are sailing on a ship to America,
but your face looks Egyptian
in the half light.

3.
You write and say you are collecting rocks
from the places you travel to.
You send me a maple leaf from Japan,
shells from Thailand, rocks from Burma and Nepal.
You know I like these things.
I tell you I feel the land from its objects.
You say that you can't,
but you will bring them to me.

You say you don't miss me,
but every place you go
you fill your room with rocks and shells.

4.
You go to the islands to get some sun
and throw your watch away.
The fisherman wakes you in the morning.
You say the fisherman's family teaches you
their language and how
to get food from the sea –
mussels, shellfish, and things you never
would have dreamed of trying to eat before.
You learn from them to be slow.
You watch the sunrise.
They feed you rice and eggs.
If you're lucky and they catch fish,
you eat something different.
They pull bananas, pineapple, and coconuts from the trees,
and later they come into my dreams.

5.
In the postcard you deny everything.
I write and say we could die tomorrow.
If you had one day left,
who would you spend it with?
What would you do?
You say, "I know you,"
but you forget everything long distance.
You write about your poems and your
red pick-up truck because you
didn't have a wagon when you were young.
You say you like the shape
of a woman against your chest,

but more than that
you like to keep your light on
until three in the morning
without asking anyone.
Sometimes, I'm sure the dwarf has won.

Between Two Languages

Keeping silent is a tactic, but really I want to talk. In Hebrew the letters look like animals or doors to a different life that I won't be going through this time.

When I was in Jerusalem, I could not talk because I didn't know the language. The family I stayed with wanted me to marry their eldest son, but I couldn't tell them if I was tired or hungry. I danced with him in the space between two languages.

All I want to do in my dreams is dance. If you want to control your dreams, Castaneda says to look at your hands. I choose to fly instead, to leap like an antelope, a gazelle – beyond gravity. I push back stars, clouds, and time to find the place where we are still dancing.

All of my dreams are about breaking rules. Seduction, graffiti, lips touching thighs filled with foreign melodies. Something dark wrestling with an angel. I plant a redwood seedling in my yard, hoping it will grow.

If I could control my dreams, you'd love me instead of walking away. You'd understand my letters even though they are in a different language. I'd abolish distance and the airport.

I was up in the air like a bird when you dropped me. My delicate frame could not withstand the impact, and I shattered between two continents.

My dreams bring me messages. Under a wide sky carved by mountains, a river of light is pouring through my dreams. I am climbing mountain trails, drinking holy water. Angels weave light into my ankles, my muscles, my legs. Hands of light over my heart.

White Butterfly

"In Chinese symbology a white butterfly symbolizes the soul of a departed loved one. A white butterfly also means angels are watching over you, and you are being protected."
- Insight into the World of Butterflies

As the sky begins to fill
with light,
a blue feather floats into my dream.

Above the cypress tree that looks like a dragon,
a white butterfly –
spirit, messenger, ghost?

On the stairs
to my Grandmother's farmhouse,
a spider's web
becomes a harp, a ladder,
the sky filling with pelicans,
a wind chime over the ocean
weaving a B-minor chord.

My Grandmother knows the healing roots,
a cup of tea
that feels like drinking a forest.

On the path from the icehouse
to the summer kitchen,
everyone I need to forgive
appears at a window.
My brother pulls a red wagon
up a long hill
as gold bricks fall out.

A hummingbird hovers over pink dianthus
in my Grandmother's garden.
I remember her hands,

the way she kneaded bread,
what she sang as she was weaving
on the hand loom in her attic.

White butterflies hover inside angel wings.
At dawn, everything dissolves
into separate worlds.

The All Night Yemenite Café

The Seduction of Bathsheba

1.
When the King saw her bathing
in the watercolor shades of evening,
dark skin and white steam rising,
scented with hyssop and chamomile,
he became obsessed with the way
the hills and valleys of her body
rose and fell
in a sacred dance of falling leaves.

In her, he worshipped
the bright orange of the lily,
the deep purple of the grape
before it is pressed into wine,
the shape of stars,
their force fields,
and the vectors that connect them
to warriors
above the hills of Jerusalem.

Later, when his servants came for her
and her husband disappeared
into a flock of goats,
the edges of the sunset blurred,
purple, dripping and surprised
over a canvas obsessed
with the blue iridescence
of tree frogs.

At midnight
the King was barefoot,
on the balcony,
pushing his way up
through a field of lilies,

brown and ochre streets in the distance,
azaleas in the alley,
goats running madly in all directions.

2.
In the beginning
she was married to the muse,
but it became hard not to touch him,
even though the goats were running
in the opposite direction,
brown and ochre in the distance.

The summer was voluptuous in its dancing.
She gave the muse a tambourine
while she painted desert flowers
and tree frogs in clay alleys.

Sometimes she danced with him,
and sometimes by herself,
after midnight
with delicate silver anklets
on her feet.

At first the music of silver
against silver
was atonal,
but it condensed into
a pointillist painting in the leaves,
transforming the pain
into music.

3.
Her dreams were half in the ice,
half underwater.
A Yemenite bride inside a band of scimitars.
A sculpture of the whirling
energy of emerging leaves.

She told the King
she would always have two lovers,
one emotional and one artistic.
But the lover and the artist began dancing.
First in small silver steps.
Later in a love dance of wild leaping.

The ice became feather thin,
patterned with feathers.
Peacock blue,
the color of longing.
Green and gold,
the color of lucid sleep.

The night was translucent with windows
as they fell through the borders of flowers,
the edges of tambourines,
and Shabazi music
in a wild and feathery leap.

She landed
the way a prima ballerina floats
down to the swans
after a lift.
His strong, muscular arms
guided her
to the molecules of paint
as they condensed

into a landscape that was wildly sensual,
vibrantly creative,
and very silent.

4.
During the eclipse
he lay on his back under eucalyptus trees
watching the shadows condense
into tiny points of light
shaped like crescent moons.

He thought he heard a warning
in the crescents of light,
the bands of shadow,
the dark hole in the sky.

On the hills above Jerusalem,
a prophet was talking to God
inside a cloud
as the rain condensed
into Babylonian cities,
a nation in exile.

5.
Centuries later, the King's bride
is still spinning watercolors
out of the edges of her dreams.
She is the ballerina with wild black hair,
the Yemenite smile,
and Russian dancer eyes.

Her people walk across the desert
to a city that has her name.
Colors flow out in earth tones
as she brushes her lips
across the thin membrane of wandering.

Goats graze on the borders
of the invisible.
Lizards skitter up the crevices
of sandstone walls.
Tree frogs disappear
underwater.

She is almost invisible
when she dances
in the Bedouin market.
Silk scarves and harem pants
the color of desert flowers
ripple like a mirage,
but the hills remember
earth tone spices in the open air,
the color of her skin.

Driving South to the Dead Sea

We were apart for more than five years, except for a hidden place where I sometimes saw you in dreams. Now, we're driving south to the Dead Sea, talking in Hebrew and English, listening to love songs on the radio.

We stop at the Bedouin Market at Be'er Sheva. I find a teapot with colors like desert flowers. A Moroccan merchant waves to me. His clay pots are shaped by hand, glazed with three shades of blue, ancient buildings of Jerusalem painted in pastels above the Temple Wall. You bargain with him, from 15 shekels to 12, and buy it for me. Later you tell me you could have gotten it for 10 if you had waited longer.

After a lunch of salads, eggplant, carrots, olives, hummus, mangos, falafel and pita at a small outdoor café, we walk around the old part of the city. The flowers on the trees are lavender and a brilliant pink. Two young men step into my photograph, thinking I want to photograph them instead of the trees. One of them pees on the wall and says, *temunah shel tachat sheli*. Picture of my ass. Maybe he thinks I don't understand.

Then we continue south to the Dead Sea, driving below sea level on land, past caves with desert animals and hidden Essene scrolls. Carved desert monuments, sandy and gold. The Dead Sea turquoise as the sky in the distance.

At night we go out on the roof of the hotel, then down an unlit stairway to the beach, where our hands are beginning to remember each other under the moonlight. The stars above us – the Bear, Cassiopeia, and a shooting star that runs halfway across the sky before it destroys itself.

My body remembers you completely. I fall into sleep in the lighted space between us, suspended between two continents. But in the middle of the night, I wake up doubting everything. My memories, my dreams, my intuition, even myself. And the window you closed before midnight. I had wanted it open.

The All Night Yemenite Café

We've been walking around Jaffa late at night,
on pilgrimage to everything
that artists want to see –
the ancient well by the art center,
walled walks below clusters of lights
like Babylonian flowers or ancient moons,
fishing boats by the harbor,
the Mediterranean Sea
and the night sky of Tel Aviv
from an elevated walkway.
Artist galleries, murals, fish restaurants,
and hidden places for kisses.

He tells me the wild crowd gathers
at Nargila, the all night Yemenite Café,
after 2:00 in the morning.
He tells the waitress we want to sit outside,
and she hands him a 12-page menu.
He opens it from the back
and shows me a picture
of a dark man and a blonde woman
feasting on each other.
He says it helps the appetite,
makes you hungry.

He turns the pages slowly
to show me erotic pictures and wild poems
between the prices of the food.
Naked women next to ancient Yemenite treats.
While our food is being cooked,
he translates an article from the *Late Evening News*
telling how the religious tried to close the place down,
but the City Council said there wasn't a law against it.
Below this, the owner's response
is framed by naked women.

He says the restaurant has two menus
and *yekes* can order from the other one.
That's an Israeli word that sort of means "nerd."
Besides, the Yemenite restaurant next door
with the regular menu is always empty.

We order eggplant, pitas,
and a Yemenite treat called *Ziva*.
It's curved like a snake
but has a woman's name.

Two 17-year-old boys come into the outdoor café.
They're laughing, looking at the menu,
reading every word,
and trying to think of something to order
so they can keep looking at the pictures.
It's 3:00 in the morning by now.
A group of tourists comes in
and asks if they have a different menu.
The waitress says, "I can give you
the one for people under fourteen."

Since it's my first time,
the waitress gives me a bumper sticker
that says, "Nargila, where they sell pleasure
and Yemenite food."
I think about putting it on my car in Iowa –
something completely wild
that the fundamentalists can't read
and wouldn't understand if they could.
But my friend says Hebrew letters
might make me a target for terrorists
even there.

The food is so spicy it makes me burn
and stirs my appetite for deeper things.
He is Yemenite too, so I bite his fingers.
Now we're hungry for dessert,
so we drive home through the almost deserted
streets of Tel Aviv
for something much better than food.
And in the morning
after three hours of sleep,
we both wake up laughing.

Better by Moonlight

"There are some flowers that bloom
Better by moonlight than in the sun."
                            - Bernard Soulie

It's one of those perfect moments –
after dark, but early enough
to have my eyes wide open,
a gibbous moon in the sky
with a halo around it,
predicting tomorrow's heat.

We leave our car by the beach,
next to a stone tower.
In the garden you show me
small yellow flowers called *Ner Ha'Laila* –
candles of the night.
The blossoms open at night
and only once.
By the morning, they're gone.

You ask me to say it with you,
Ner Ha'Laila.

We walk by the sand dunes
arm in arm
to a place where
hundreds of people are dancing
on the beach
samba and lambada
some in uniform
some younger
all of them wild.

The lights of Jaffa
are amber in the distance
as we walk back.

When you pull me
close to you
the music still lifts us
like the white birds we saw
flying in slow circles
above the Mediterranean Sea.

Bright yellow flowers
are blooming between the stones,
their supernova petals
stronger than the stars
I can cover with my fingers.

You call me *Ner Ha'Laila,*
your Middle Eastern dancer,
your Japanese temple fire
late at night.

You open my petals,
drop ripples
into the place where
the sky is born.

I am the flower that blooms
only for you
only at night
and
only once.

By morning, it's gone.

Gifts

A small opening
between us
in the shadows we reflect
on the wall –
a heart, a bone.

We play tag in the water,
and I keep
letting him catch me.

I show him photographs –
dark hair falling
past my shoulders,
slender legs
wrapping around a cello,
and he remembers.

He points
to where I was looking
when the music stopped
and says, *In the balcony–*
I was listening
up here.

Pale blue jeans
softly sculptured
on the floor.

I trace the bones
connected
like wings
behind his shoulders
with my smallest finger.

Now the sun
is rising at Stonehenge.
I feel the light
on my lips.

Photograph from Okinawa

In the photograph
she is coming down the stairs
from the bath house where she lives.
You are the 19-year-old Marine
from North Carolina
whose words flow into her ears
like an exotic song
from the other side of a mystery.

You are tall, handsome
and the wide muscles of your arms
push into the seams of your shirt
before you scatter your uniform
on her tatami floor.

She is lost in the cornflower blue
of your eyes as you rock
her narrow bed
and fill the halls of the bath house
with cat sounds.

And in the geisha curves
of her perfect island body
you are trying to forget the daylight
of the military base
where you don't have a voice.

When you ask her to smile
for the photograph
you don't notice the way
her eyes are glazing over the pain
she feels every time she remembers
the soldier who went to Vietnam
and exploded one afternoon

in the middle of the jungle
in a cloud of orange fire.

And you are unaware
that moments before you leave this island
for the last time
she will try to fold herself
in your suitcase.

A week later
two of your friends will tell you
that they found her at midnight
running naked down the street.

When they bring her back
to the bath house
she will dream she is eight years old,
trying to dig a tunnel to North Carolina
with a silver spoon.

She has no idea
that twenty years later
after your round-eye wife
breaks all of your dishes
and walks out of your house
for the last time,
after your next girlfriend
is dragged out of her apartment in Manhattan,
tied up, and thrown into a suitcase,
after five pilgrimage journeys
to holy places in the Himalayas
at altitudes beyond where
the people you've left behind can breathe,
and the other woman you have finally come to love

walks out of your house for the last time
and won't even answer your phone calls,
you will find her photograph.

She doesn't know
that you worship her now
inside a golden frame
beside your paintings of bodhisattvas
and holy stones from the Ganges River.

She has no idea
how much you loved her,
and you didn't either
at the time.

Wild Orchids

I want to think of the men I love
like stones I find at the beach –
the ones at Año Nuevo
at the private beach
beyond the "No Trespassing" sign.
That's where you find the rocks
with the seashell fossils
in a secret place.

I want to be able to pick them up
and put them down
without sorrow,
like a wild orchid
I leave where it is growing.

That would be the way
to let go
like a starfish or a moonshell,
curved, spotted like a leopard,
floating on a rivulet through the sand
all the way out to the ocean –
letting go
the way the Buddhist monks
I met high up in the mountains in Nepal
taught me.

The echo of your face still orbits around me
like a familiar planet.
I can't forget
the blue grey of your eyes
full of fear and longing,
your arms
reaching for me
from the center of an Egyptian prayer,

your strong legs
with muscles curved like shells,
and the "No Trespassing" sign.

In the late hours of the evening,
I surround myself with words.
They fill up with salt water and sing,
and they make me strong.

I learn so much from my failures
that I have to bless them.
Sometimes I think we are all
intricate patterns of shell inside rock,
glowing with the memory of ancient lives.

I want to be waist high
in calla lilies,
up to my elbows
in birds of paradise
orange as the California sun
on a path leading out to the ocean
just before sunrise.
I want to sing
until I forget
the meaning of sorrow.

How to Jumpstart a Dream

1.
Rainbow ribbons are rippling
in a wind
formed by a vortex of dreams.

Look for something hanging
by a window,
a Japanese fern,
banners with messages
or lead crystals.

Blow into them.
Create movement
before you dissolve into the vision
on the other side.

2.
Look for the reflection of tiny stars
in an amethyst crystal,
and watch the delicate
points of light
move
as you step backwards.

Line up geodes
at the foot of your bed.

Find the color missing
from the rainbow
reflected by a hidden light,
and follow it
until the asteroid particles
blur.

3.
Follow the images in your photographs
into the light of a foreign country.
Cross over a suspended bridge
to the Kali Gandaki River gorge
and walk on the other side
of the river.

Follow a row of prayer flags
into the air.

Pose asymmetrically
on top of a mountain in Tibet
and follow the spindrift
up to the moon.

4.
Rub oils scented with jasmine
or coconut
into your skin.
Follow the edges
of your elbows and knees,
the scent of a balmy wind
blowing up from the south.

Angels with glass wings will guide you.
Ask them questions,
even if you can't see them.

Use your pinky
to trace a spiral on your belly.
Listen for melodies
in the musical curve in the small
of your back.

Follow the half moons
on both sides of your heart
into the sky.

5.
Light a beeswax candle
inside the tin lantern
that reflects snowflakes all over the sky
of the silent place where you sleep.

Put cinnamon, cardamom, ginger
into your midnight tea.
Drink it slowly
and follow the winding journey
of the water
as it melts into your body.

Let your edges expand
into snowflakes
as you melt into sleep.

6.
Put your left hand softly
over the spinning wheel of your heart
and fall asleep
loving all the unfinished places
of your journey into the unknown.

When you wake up
another piece of what
you have been searching for
will fly into your throat
softly, like a bird
made of starlight.

Sing back to her
before you turn the corner
behind the mirror.

The Winter Life of Shooting Stars

Parachute

I am crawling through a parachute. It's a tunnel of gauze or silk or ripstop, with Persephone pushing my knees. I am blindfolded with a green silk scarf. Or maybe it's purple. Isadora's dancers or dragonflies push my body into distortions. I am wild inside gauze. Spinning inside air. Crawling in the dark toward a flicker of light. It's a mystery covered by a cocoon while meteor showers explode over my shoulders.

There aren't any instructions, and I'm surrounded by ripstop. I'm free falling from the air with prayer flags drifting around my ankles. Floating in the dark. Yellow and black stripes of light and shadow drift across my feet. Banded bees are trying to tell me stories, but all I hear is a buzzing in my ears. I am rolling down a long green hill a long time ago. I am picking a wild bouquet of poppies for my second grade teacher.

I am walking the high beams of new houses abandoned by the carpenters of the late afternoon. The last farm stopped giving pumpkins in October, but this is a good place to collect discarded nails with my 8-year-old friends. The beams are an open theater, and the shadows tell us stories. We have borrowed our mothers' scarves, and we are teaching the bees how to dance.

My lover and I are dancing barefoot after midnight. We are both covered with oil inside a steam of jasmine flowers. I skate counterclockwise over his body before the second hand stops. We might be in Kyoto or Tel Aviv, but the walls are now a blur. My heart is shaking, or maybe it is the walls.

The tunnel is streaming with gauze as I crawl in the semi-dark. The bees are humming softly on the other side of the parachute. The tone is silk or translucent, and floating. It's a new kind of music that I refused to listen to before. The bees say the erotic is in the shadows, and nobody can love without the wound. They tell me we all need to be pierced to know the mystery.

I am dancing inside a parachute, and suddenly I don't know how to fall. I am high above a Ferris wheel of strangers, a thousand paper cranes after the bomb explodes at Hiroshima. The sake, still warm from the heat of your hands, is spilling across the table while you paint on my back with ink-covered fingers.

There is someone whose collarbone I see in my dreams. He sings to me in bass harmonic overtones in a familiar language. I can almost hear him breathing while poppies grow through the cracks in the slate path. I meet him in the tunnels between the pyramids.

Angel of Eros

Montreal thunderstorm.
Jazz ripping through water
in the minor key of the
late afternoon.

He's been avoiding her
in the shiver of the current
of the stream that flows north
through his land,
in the deer tracks buried
under the fence
before it falls down in a blizzard,
in the cows that escaped two weeks ago
from his neighbor's farm.
But now his scent is melting
through her hair.

He is greedy for these words,
but she keeps them covered.

She tells him to keep the white room empty.
The shelves he built so carefully
are not for his books.
It's a place where the future vibrates
in holographic messages,
a tunnel from the hieroglyphs
underground.

She runs her fingers along the lines
of his cheekbones,
shaving bark.
The music evaporates
like oak leaves dissolving under water.

In the open room
the humid air settles
like the density of a desire
that is still invisible.
The only furniture
is the atonal harmony
of a cello weaving through water.

The only voice
is the finger that ripples
down his spine and whispers
keep the room empty.

Gypsy Honeymoon

First your voice came.
Then the photograph.

I am meeting you from the inside out.

Even before I see you,
I might be stroking the fine
hair of your forearms with my words,
running the soft edges of my hands
along your ankles,
or kissing the whisper of your collarbone.

I know that bone –
I saw it in a dream.

If I open the lighthouse,
can you stand the intensity
of silver fish swimming to the moon?

Right now it is midnight.
Two lovers are kissing on top of a stone wall
as their shadows stretch across a gypsy garden.
They walk through wild asparagus,
lupines, opium poppies,
mountain trails of wild irises.

Rhododendron petals
float to their bare
feet over stones.

It is only moments before I see you.

Right now we are picking wild blackberries.
Right now we are the happiest people in the world.

The Winter Life of Shooting Stars

When you wrestle with an angel
and try to overcome her,
you get wounded.
— Dorit Har

1.

When winter came
I ran out of your words.
I couldn't even find them dreaming.
Your words became a genetic code
hidden inside sunflowers
and shooting stars.

Above the northern border
your voice spread like a supernova,
a shower of first snow,
but I was too far south
to pick up the frequency.

Strangers called you on the telephone,
and your words tumbled like water,
tumbled naked
on the rocks, silver
inside streams of falling stars.

You wanted to give yourself
only to yourself or distant strangers,
a Bodhisattva of the radio.
Now you belong to everyone,
especially your voice.

2.

We are riding on a train through Northern Ireland.
We travel through a field of dinosaur bones
and prehistoric war horses.

A woman I don't know
is singing in the post office,
her voice as sweet as a sunflower,
all of us waiting for messages
or sending paper airplanes
to places we can't see,
as if people in other countries
could love us more
than we love ourselves.

As if her voice
could make the snow melt
before its time.

A comet arcs below
the Big Dipper.
Through my telescope
the particles distort and blur,
focus and separate.

You are still in Canada
hiking on trails that cross
a frozen river,
lost inside a room of
Persian carpets.

Locked in my own silence,
I have become a hologram
naked
in a mountain spring
surrounded by silver stones.

3.

After the first snow,
I dance to the music of
a violinist who knows how to travel
between stars
with a partner who can't see
my home.

His glasses form a border
around his face,
a fence around the meteor showers,
a cage for the wildness.

I am lost inside a crowded room.
Someone whose voice I only heard once
in a field of lavender
slides in behind me,
pulls me to his chest,
and I melt into his voice.

His hands trace the definition
of muscles under silk.
Under white dancer's tights,
a suggestion of soft petals.
But I don't know where this dance
is leading.

4.

The clock is a night light.
At 2:00 in the morning
it is twenty years ago.
I am teaching children how to swim
inside the belly of a whale
with a glass window.
Every two weeks
we send up helium balloons
with postcards tied to a string.

I am watching a sky full of
red blue green and yellow
balloons
disappear into the late afternoon.
Maybe I'll get a postcard from the Pleiades.

Here is the message:
"If you find me,
    tell me where I'm from
        and mail me back."

5.

The snow falls under a street lamp
in a city where I haven't lived
for twenty years.
Or is the sand
shifting in layers around
the pyramid walls?

Sometimes I think that life is a singing lesson.
Hitting the right note is intuitive
and mysterious.

I haven't heard your name,
but I see you in hologram –
the tendril of your collarbone,
the neon blue ice trail
of a shooting star.

Black and White Photograph

His house is hidden in the woods
by a thicket of walnut trees.
The only sign of life –
two white buckets
leaning together like lovers
in the left corner of the
photograph.

He speaks to me in f-stops:
the sink full of copper pots
and bottles of antique glass,
the wood-burning stove from the 1800s,
the bicycle
leaning under the bedroom window
with handlebars that already
have become vines.

He says, "the subtle shades
are what bring out the luminosity."

Everything is light and shadow –
the edges of late afternoon sunlight
inside bottles distracting
the vertical lines of his windows,
the shadows of elderberry
leaves waving above the violets
when sunlight comes from the backs of things,
wood fences falling into the landscape,
sunflowers lit from within.

He says, "In the camera's eye,
you are looking at the back of your own retina.
You are swimming in a world of light."

The low range brings the shadows luminous –
a clutter of branches under his window
with fingers reaching for blackberries
under a ripple of hand-rolled glass.
The high range highlights only.
Shadows fall into the valley
of unfinished dreams.

There are images I can't capture –
the scent of deer musk,
the printer's muscled forearms,
and the slanted light on the printing press
folding shadows.
The pile of his grandmother's dishes,
and the silver goblets
waiting for hands.

He closes the bathroom door,
draws a thick curtain over the window,
fills the lion's paw tub
with trays of Kodak developer,
stop bath,
finishing rinse to erase
the edges of water.

In the dark
we watch the images appear –
pure metallic silver
blooming like sunflowers.

I would like to adjust my life
to the shutter speeds of a camera –
slower subject with the sky deeply blue,

cottony puffs of thunder clouds
hanging low in the eastern sky
above the slats on the porch swing,
and the dancer with luminous hands
still touching the sparrow's wing.

Everything is light and shadow –
long rows of summer corn
just above my shoulders,
a bee's wing,
the waving petals of sunflowers,
the whole world blooming, everything
lit from within.

Beyond the Walls

I walk into a synagogue in Poland.
It is fifty years ago – before I was born.
The men are in a large
room with white
shawls over their shoulders.
The edges are fringed like sheaves of wheat
or snow falling between branches of olive trees.
The women pray in a balcony to the side.
It's warm there – like soup.
The light is the color of soft candles.
They invite me into their circle of song.

I am standing outside the western
wall of the Temple in Jerusalem.
It is 2000 years ago.
We are carrying sheaves of wheat
over our shoulders
as an offering to God.
We are a human river of white robes
and sandals, with flecks of wheat falling
into the sunlight around our feet.
Around us, the cadence of prayer,
a prophecy, a thunder cloud.
We enter the gate to the outer
wall and dance inside with our wheat,
shaking it in all six directions.
But the mystery in the center is closed.

There is fighting in front of David's Tower,
outside the Jaffa Gate.
Too many soldiers from I don't know where.
Suddenly, I am floating
in the air above the temple walls.
I am higher than the crows

who lay their eggs above the temple walls,
higher than the doves who hover
over the Mediterranean Sea.
I am filled with love and light,
and I can speak to God directly
as though he is my closest friend.
Suddenly, I know the mystery
inside the Holy of Holies.

Violins of Hope

*The Violins of Hope are a collection of fifty string
instruments once played by Jewish prisoner-musicians
in the camps and ghettos of the Holocaust.*

"Wherever there were violins, there was hope."
- James A. Grymes

Bright star
northern lights
above ancient skies
in the invisible dark,
a prayer for one more day
of miracles.

On the train
from Terezin to Auschwitz
hope died
in the cattle cars
and the cloud of cyanide,
stone soap
bright stars extinguished.
But light embracing hope
endures
in the memories
of the wood.

Visions of the sunrise
in his heart,
but the light was hidden
below the rhythm of trains rumbling
down the tracks.

From the deepest part
of memory,
an owl is calling
to the infinite silence.
Pastel colors swirl
into a painting of the sky.

The violinist
was old enough to feel
everything – the sigh of the strings,
the trembling in the vibrato
the minor key of
the future
with every sweep of his bow.

Each note was a prayer,
his hands
shaping notes
the way he used to touch his wife,
embracing trees
holding time, stars and atoms
with strings and wood
from enchanted forests.

In the Voices of the Birds

What I most remember about Christopher
is the way he knew the names
of all the birds
at dawn
by their songs.

His cornsilk blonde hair
blue overalls, no shirt
the strength of his shoulders
and the way we stayed awake all night.

There was light in his touch
between the birds.
They flew in and out
of his fingers,
and birds outside our window –
a window we couldn't
open again that way.

We met when we could after that,
in Iowa, Switzerland, San Francisco,
in borrowed cabins by two different oceans.
You took me to my brother's wedding
in a red pick-up truck,
made fun of the priest and his future
mother-in-law,
which you claimed permission to do
because you were Catholic.

I remember the way you hurt me,
what you said,
and the sentence I typed on your
portable Smith Corona in Nantucket
before I left
for the last time.

It was November,
with a light dusting of snow
over the sand.
The pebbles on the beach
hid their messages.

On separate sides of the continent
we listened to different oceans
and slammed our lives shut –
you in Brooklyn Heights
with your two-year-old son
on your shoulder,
me in San Francisco
climbing the long hill
to 24th Street.

Twelve years later,
holding your first book of poems
in my hands, I am
hungry for memories,
hungry for every word,
hungry for any hint of a message
where I might find myself.

In the inscription, you write
"There are histories
in this book you may
be familiar with, because
you were there."

I am not the arms
where you will rest your head
when you're eighty years old,
but I always hear you
in the voices of the birds.

WALTZ

The comet discovers a blue path
over your shoulder,
spinning through outer space
above the wood porch railing.

We are whirling to the harmonies of
"Star of the County Down,"
your arm in the midheaven
of my back, holding
burgundy velvet.
A violin is weaving through
the flute,
but your eyes hold me to
a deeper melody.

Around the borders of
my seeing, your hair
curls into a halo of memory.
Maybe it is the full moon
or the thunder clouds gathering
out of season
over the rolling Wisconsin
cow pastures
predicting tomorrow's snow.

As we circle around each other,
the wind swirls over
the red barn
next to the 19th century
school house,
a terrifying beauty
that will blow the walls apart.

If I invite you into my house,
I know you would take the time

to find the trilobites
and the seashell fossils,
to see how the curve of the cello
fits my leg.
I'd watch you fold the prayers
you have almost forgotten
into saffron wrapped around
the bare feet of the Buddha.

And in your eyes
I might find the blue imprint
of a comet,
a message from a planet
near the Pleiades
etched by a ten-year-old
with a switchblade
into your largest finger,
an almost forgotten memory
of the way back home.

Entering the Word Temple

My Mother's Daughter

It is five years before I was born,
before life ruined her.

She is sixteen years old,
breasts rising like yeasted bread
which she tries to conceal on the streets
of her immigrant neighborhood,
but when she sings in night clubs,
she stuffs her dress with tissues,
paints her lips red,
and styles her hair like Judy Garland.

At Weequahic High School
she joins the hall patrol
to station herself outside the door
of my father's sixth period class.
She's smiling every afternoon
when he walks out of the door.

Later they escape to the West Village
in his red convertible
to the apartment he shares with his half brother
in a loft filled with etchings.

When he walks into the night club
where she pretends to be eighteen years old,
she sings to my father
directly with bedroom eyes,
How High the Moon
blasting out of Tommy's trombone
and then cascading from her mouth.
Who could resist such a song?

By the subway stop to Harlem
to see Billie Holiday,
he buys two gardenias for her hair.

A few months later,
they hitchhike to a cabin
by Caroga Lake in upstate New York,
share a bottle of wine,
throw the glasses into the fire
and create me.

Years later, my mother will tell me how
I ruined her career,
but she has a transparent face.
In the photograph
in the small apartment in Spanish Harlem
where they lived after I was born,
I see her completely happy.

Visions from the Right Hand of the Madonna

1.
She brought me fresh baked bread
with rye flour, walnuts and onions
still warm from the oven.
In the heat I could feel her love.

It's been difficult to eat
but the bread says
look to the future.

It's in the scent of the onions
and the wheat. Inside
the skin of the tangerines
in the basket by my window.

2.
I dream about a man with angel hands
who touches with such ethereal tenderness
that he almost doesn't belong to this place.
He seems to be far away
from the pain of this planet.

The oil he massages into
my back and shoulders
is scented with lilacs.
I can feel love pouring out
from his fingertips,
but even the love seems to be
from somewhere else.

His hands spread visions across my skin
at the base of my spine
where hummingbirds build their nests.

Further north, the music
of breaking icicles
falls while the snow bear
walks over a shadow of the moon.

On the other side of the tunnel,
the aurora is turquoise
with polar bears walking
on the ice floe.

A river of turquoise light
is flowing through my body.
I don't know if he is an angel
or a tantric magician,
but the roof is gone now.

The moon is a white lantern
in Kyoto
above the geisha district of Gion.

In the light
that floats between the bare branches
of plum trees,
I am walking down narrow alleys
toward the teahouse.

3.
In the alley beside my house
I burn letters
in three different languages.

Across the continent
two towers are falling
near the place of my birth.
In the minds of the people who live there,
they fall again and again.

But on the altar
in front of the church
that is home for the rescue workers,
people from all places
bring poems, sculpture, photographs,
a bronze dancing Shiva inside a circle of flowers,
Indonesian finger puppets, tribal masks from Africa,
blue and yellow banners from firemen,
the Black Madonna, yellow roses,
crayon posters from school children,
Our Lady of Guadalupe
and an ancient Hebrew blessing.

Every morning the women
bring new roses
even though three months later,
the ground is still smoking.
The memory falls in
smoke so thick you can't
see out to your hand,
a banner painted by school children
draped over the fence
at the edge of the graveyard.

But somewhere else,
three degrees to the right of feminine,
an angel rides a green donkey
to the moon, tossing flowers
to the aurora.

Venus of the Birds

She disappeared on a Thursday
in the evening with a stranger
and a dream of Monarch butterflies,
leaving her bare wood floors
for Wisconsin or California.
She didn't leave a message
or a note for her friends –
only shampoo and a bicycle
in the middle of an empty room.
Only the echo of Chinese vases,
bottles of herbs,
and two Tibetan bells.

When she swam in *Lago di Como*
the boats turned. The fishermen
came closer to see
the young woman swimming
toward the island in a white bikini
while fish flapped in wooden buckets.
When she kneeled in churches,
statues spoke to her.
In the late afternoon
she walked in the piazza,
weaving between the restless crowds
of young Italian men.
One of them wanted her to go with him,
but she couldn't speak the language.
She didn't know how to say
yes, or no.

In the afternoons, she rode her bicycle
into the fields, searching for wildflowers,
a perfect lavender calyx,
a field of tiger lilies

with tangerine four o'clock light
shining through the petals.
She wanted to learn the language of birds,
the chant of the meadowlark,
the blue arc of the barn swallow,
Canada geese flying home.

She always felt like a stranger,
even in her dreams.
At midnight she cocoons herself
inside a circle of candles,
tones with Tibetan bells
to invent a new language.
In her garden she plants
watermelon, comfrey and zucchini,
her melon breasts swimming at the edge
of her white muslin blouse.

She stops eating, except for herbs
and juice from the vegetables
she grows in her garden,
but her father won't disappear,
especially in the dreams
where she harvests lightning.
She has to go away.
By her window
a tangerine sweater tossed over a chair,
blackberry vines stretching
to a sliver moon.

Her friends search their dreams for visions,
ask for messages from the birds.
Outside, behind the barn
a cluster of black-eyed Susans.

A hummingbird hovers, flies low,
but escapes my hand.
Perhaps she has become a butterfly.
I hope she is in Wisconsin
or California,
face lifted to the sky, her voice a breeze
through the petals of sunflowers.
I can almost see her
filling an empty room with wildflowers,
a candle and a painted flute,
searching for her own music
to whisper to the birds.

Autumn in Iowa

I stuff I Ching pennies
into a parking meter.
The sun tilts through colored glass,
turns blue in my kitchen window.

We put on costumes for Halloween.
I dance after midnight
with a bare-chested man
with boxing gloves.

The peony stalks are brittle
in the wind, and the coneflowers
have turned brown before November.
Field mice bury their fur
inside the quiet places of the heart.

MERIDIANS

Love is not an emotion.
Love is who you are.

1.
His hands told her
that he was one of the Tantric sculptors
of the Temple in Varanasi
where Hindu gods and goddesses
are perpetually making love.

Halfway around the world,
he traces the fire meridian
up her left leg.

The butterfly angel who dances
out of her heart chakra
has flame blue swallowtail
wings.

2.
Men are the sea she swims in.
In the Temple in Varanasi
or on the basketball floor of the gym
at the 43rd and Judah
contra dance
in San Francisco.

She walks through the door
with a red pashmina shawl
draped around her shoulders.

Men are the sea she swims in
under floating summer light
when she dances
face to open face

with her eyes burning
a soft trail of fire.

He says,
"Let me be a soft cocoon
for you." He takes
her spinning through
soft blue light. He would
like to know the mystery.

During the silent prayer
she envisions his face –
blue pearl eyes,
the wide arc of his mouth,
his compassionate
face.

3.
She holds the sheets to her skin
wraps herself inside them
so she can breathe his molecules again.

An echo of burgundy satin
in the shape of the
ballgown she wore,

a single violet
fooled by November warmth
into blooming,

the room where they danced
now empty except for
the echo of a flute.

4.
The location is nowhere,
something exotic, foreign
something more musical than linguistic.

His hands emerge
from inside a sculpture of lovers
carved centuries ago,
beauty without a filter.

Halfway around the world
the sky is clear night after night,
Pegasus and the Pleiades
floating above
a long arc of milky stars.

The sky is open, transparent
except for the evening
of the Leonid Meteor showers
and his voice
outside her window.

At 4:00 in the morning,
he is tapping on her window.
"Wake up! Shine!
Come with me and see
the stars flying across the sky!
Sing to me! Don't be afraid."

5.
She dreams she is a hummingbird
and she needs to fly
in the morning.

Her voice sings inside the sculpture
of the Temple at Varanasi,
beauty without a filter.

When she dances,
she discovers something about herself,
silver bells
wrapped around her ankles,
and the music comes from everywhere.

In another world
the contralto singing of a tamboura
and hands that teach her more deeply
who she is and where
she is located
on the Earth meridian.

Every time he speaks
a hummingbird
flies out of his mouth

And you have to
walk through fire
to go anywhere in her house.

Virgins in the Uffizi

In the morning she said she was tired
of seeing naked men.
We were in *Firenze,* walking to
the *Piazza della Signori*
on the way to the Uffizi,
which she called the penis museum.
She had just turned eighteen
with her hair still in braids
like the Botticelli maiden
speaking flowers.

An aging Italian goddess
leads us through corridors of
Giotto, Botticelli, Leonardo
with a sense of humor.
She says that Michaelangelo's paintings
are really sculptures in two dimensions
and asks us to pay attention to the way
Titian and Caravaggio use paint to capture light.

She discusses how Renaissance art
went back to the earlier gods, resurrected
the light in the human body.
It's inspiring, overwhelming,
but after two days of naked marble men,
my eighteen-year-old friend
finds herself looking at men on the street
the wrong way.

In the afternoon we walk to
Boboli Gardens at *Palazzo Pitti,*
pay homage to Venus of the Birds.
The pigeons can make a fool of anything
including sculpted marble.

They sit on the head of Adonis,
peck at Hercules' shoulders,
nest on Neptune's uncovered private parts.
They tease Diana and bite her fingers.

My braided friend throws bread
to glowing silver carp in the dirty pond.
A pregnant cat rubs against her knees
while Venus gazes forever at Adonis
in this Florentine Eden.
On the other side of the railing,
a moat, pomegranates, fig trees,
and raked gravel walkways
that humans are not allowed to enter.

By the pond, pigeons are speaking
to the gods of Eden.
They fly from frog to peacock
at the feet of a water nymph.
On the hills of *Firenze*,
rows of olive trees
and relics of too many wars.
The clouds are puffed tortellini
sliced carelessly
over an Eden of orange and lemon trees.

We walk back on streets from earlier centuries,
but crossing the bridge at *Ponte Vecchio*
a man with eyes made for a movie
catches hers. She is drawn to the sculpture
of his high Roman cheekbones,
the charm of his curly Italian hair
and a few words of broken English.
She wonders how it might be

to run off with him somewhere. And words
are not the only language.

In the evening, she decides not to go
to see the statue of David.
Enough is enough, and Michaelangelo
can wait until she is older.
But *Firenze* is full of statues.
At the end of any shaded walkway
always lovers embracing,
but that will come later.

Entering the Word Temple

1. Bird Face

A lacework of yellow oak leaves
in front of the porch of a woman
who paints visions on the walls.

Her colors are from a different place.

The man in her vision has wings
flying over the city of music
with the face of an Egyptian
mythological bird.

The city has a sand bridge
over a blue river.

If she paints him,
he will find her.

2. Amethyst Birds

Around her windows
he painted amethyst birds
flying to South America.

He hid photographs under her pillow
while the house became
lantern green and violet.

Autumn was unseasonably warm.
The wind came from South America,
made his body strong with desire
and conflicted longing.

Hundreds of ladybugs flew
in through the cracked windows.
She counted the spots on their wings.

Now, everything in her house
is covered by a thin layer of dust –
even the glass hummingbird
in her dreams.

3. Bear Song

As the season changes
the edges of the leaves
are on fire.

The Earth is getting colder,
entering the empty space.

In a loft apartment
a cello
a single note
of a Bach partita
the cadence of an Italian song.

Each day
I find the single note
that vibrates.

4. Snow Dream

The snow comes out of season,
swirling around a wrought-iron street lamp
twenty years ago.

I wake up from a dream
of pelicans and flamingos.
My skin is rose pink.

I am running barefoot
on a beach of smooth stones.

I am in the air –
a butterfly, a meadowlark,
an open window.

5. Walking over the Bridge

My memories fill with sunlight and sand
tinted the colors of a Tibetan mandala.

I find sand in unexpected places.
Inside a vase of swirled blue glass.

Falling out of sand dollars.
Inside hiking socks with a memory
of the Pacific Ocean.

We walk over a wood bridge
after midnight. In the sky
Orion shoots his arrow
with sand falling out of his belt.

6. Chrysanthemums

The cold is delayed.
In November, pink chrysanthemums
still blooming.

My house is layered with new colors –
lavender, purple and lantern green,
what I see inside
the colors of music.

Beyond the open window
the edges of the leaves –
a river of earth and sky
spinning like Sufi women
surrounded by morning glories
and galaxies.

7. Cello Lesson

In the middle of the forest
I am wearing a black velvet gown.

Muddy print of leaves
on a hidden path,
an amethyst, an echo, a memory.

Inside a grove of pine trees
he plays the cello,
gives his music to the trees.
The song he plays
is for me.

The kiss surprises me.

Music from the pyramids.
Secrets burned
inside the Alexandrian Fire.

Red squirrel
walking on thin branches
through an open window.

Ascending

For Grandma Helen

I like to think of her up there
with my grandfather,
standing in a field sweet with blossoming roses,
white corn, cucumbers and tomatoes on the vine
above the clouds.

I see her standing in grey suede pumps
and a tailored suit,
the way she looked when I was a girl,
holding my grandfather's hand.
By her heels her two dogs,
Gretchen and Frieda,
a lazy group of dappled cows grazing
in the green and shimmering
distance.

We spread out the linen table cloth
she wove on the loom in her attic
for a picnic, her basket overflowing
with herbs and flowers from the hills,
a bottle of red Italian wine,
bread she baked and goat cheese.
We are humming African melodies,
with a spiral of a cloud
wisping above the mountain.

My grandmother is weaving
a linen of sky and clouds,
the blue thread like a jet stream
expanding into the shimmering
dawn. She is gazing up at a dragonfly,
the arc of the dew beaded on
a morning glory leaf
in the early morning sunlight.

Two Shepherd puppies chase each other
between the meadowlarks.
For a moment, she has forgotten everything
except how to sing.

In the summer kitchen, my grandmother
is canning green tomatoes
with the recipe she learned
when she was nine years old
from great-grandmother Lena.
She is slicing onions, stirring a marinade of
dill seeds, brown sugar, and cider vinegar.

My brothers and I
are sunning ourselves on the dock
of the pond that seemed so big to us.
We are swimming in black inner tubes
to cool ourselves from the summer sun,
dragonflies skimming the water
inside a cacophony of bullfrogs.

Grandma Helen, we toast to you
with goblets of Merlot –
my brothers, my father, my mother,
everyone who held you dear –
as you walk through a field of tiger lilies.
This spring I am planting pink dianthus
and sunflowers in my garden –
flowers you loved so much,
black dirt sifting through my hands
as I bless you.

Market Street Angel

*"Approach pain and suffering
with curiosity and tenderness"
– Buddhist Saying*

Mostly rich people go to the Symphony.
At the pre-concert talk, the conductor
calls the canon we will hear
a musical handshake across six centuries.
He says if you listen closely,
the music will reveal its secrets.
The violins swell like ocean waves,
green and crashing through the moon.

The conductor is an acrobat, an astronaut,
a genius, but in the second tier
the sound is too small.
My friend who plays trumpet for other concerts
leans over the balcony
to get closer, and I wonder
what would happen here in an earthquake.

After the symphony,
a homeless man with chocolate eyes
reminds me of a saint, except
he wants something from you.
No. No. Not pears or oranges. Please money.
And Karla, the woman
who sings at the BART station,
has gotten too thin.
The sores on her face have crescendoed,
and she looks suddenly
ten years older.

On the streetcar, an old Chinese woman
moves closer to the door
to escape from the drunk

who reeks of urine.
They all live in my neighborhood
and will be riding the 71
to the end of the line,
where Mama Ocean's ebb and flow
drift in through the open skylight.

At the Haight Street circus,
19-year-olds with shaved heads,
henna tattoos and pierced navels
wait for nothing at the corner.
By the Red Victorian Theatre,
a giraffe woman in 7-inch
leopard spike heels
wears a leather miniskirt that reveals
too many secrets.

Karla, with sores on her face,
has migrated from the BART station.
She gets on the 71
to spend a night at the beach.
Like anyone who lives on the street,
all of her secrets are gone.

She rolls out her sleeping bag
on the sand
where a Goddess Moon
shines her light on everyone.
Her body is holding on
to a thin row of stars
that is leaving for the Pleiades.
Her voice is already on
a distant journey, but she sings
until 3:00 in the morning.

Tennis Ballet

In my fantasy, they aren't wearing shirts. It's later in the afternoon, cooler, and the light is pushing toward rose pink.

The Russian Dancer and the Postman volley a tennis ball. They are playing just for me. They shake hands, spin the racket. The Russian gets the serve. He lifts, dancing, flamboyant, almost fragmented. He is the Norse God Tyr, the God of Fire and Triathlon. On his feet, Nikes, the Greek Goddesses of Victory and Commercialism.

The Postman warms up slowly, saving his fire for later. He says he is out of practice, with a deceptive smile. He is a lithe and lanky animal, a panther with black fur and eyes that only see after midnight. But when the ball moves toward him, he is intensely focused.

The Russian Dancer is more interested in ballet than athletics. He leaps, pirouettes, returns the serve. Suddenly a broken string. Now, the ball is over the fence. The dancer circles, turns back. He is looking for lost sheep on the hills of Jerusalem.

A wasp hovers into a scrap of light drifting between two trees, gets into attack mode. The Postman delivers a topspin lob, way up in the air, impossible to return. A buzzing circles around me. I have to move quickly, into the shadows.

The Russian Dancer has become a philosopher of drop shots and underspins. He is a sculptor of the unlikely angle. It's more important than winning. He is Plato in the world of ideal forms. Underneath appearances is the most beautiful shot in the world.

The Russian Dancer knows that tricky shots are for flirting, and he doesn't save them. He has become a flamingo with slick pink feathers, one eye on the ball, the other watching me. After he serves the ball, his beak is in his feathers, but the Postman returns everything. They are in the Acropolis – warriors who need each other to pursue excellence. For thousands of years, it's the same conversation. A world where a difficult ball is a compliment.

The tennis ball is a woman with a wide papaya mouth, cutting melons in the Philippines. The Postman is a rock musician, with a grandstand of invisible bystanders going wild. He's on stage, and the red-winged blackbirds are swooning. The local butterflies are going wild. But he is not chasing women – he's chasing tennis balls.

In China two monk philosophers are studying the Tao. It's a philosophy of delicate calibrations, slight adjustments. In the slanted light, two dragonflies swirl around Chinese calligraphy. The words ripple. The world as they know it is about to disappear. In the late afternoon, the words disintegrate. The Universe has become round. The monks are two cicadas arcing over the ecliptic, a Southern wind full of heat and flowers in their face. The tennis ball is a hen house just before a tornado.

Bees fly to the yellow globe, circle the woman watching from the side. They almost get her. The Russian says, "That's enough violence for one afternoon," but the Postman stops hiding and slices the ball. The dancer can't return it. The ball is a flying cloud, and the sun is almost blinding in the four o'clock heat.

The Russian Dancer plays to the audience, shoulders bare, the tennis ball his excuse for a pirouette. The Postman, hiding a smile, wild eyes, Irish cheekbones, plays for himself. At the edge of the field, a bumblebee, a hummingbird, a single falling leaf. At the edge of his mind, a fantasy of a grand jeté.

The tennis ball is six wives, leaping for him at the same time, and he doesn't want any of them. They are dancing for him in a marble pool. A Sufi dancer with long dark hair covers herself with jasmine blossoms and lets the veils fall, one by one. She is spinning into a rapture. He yawns, takes off his shoes, and silently dances out the back door.

It's different in my fantasy. A volley of Norwegian shoulders, Irish cheekbones, tennis and ballet. The Russian Dancer leaping across the stage, the Postman playing a tribal beat on the bass guitar. A hot wind blows in from Africa. In the distance, a singular falling leaf, a butterfly, a plié. The tennis ball flying at the speed of a fighter jet. The butterfly, an ascending note of a Bach partita, in and out of the chain link fence. My heart is a faded half moon over an elderberry branch, snowing blossoms.

The Russian Dancer flirts with the butterfly, slices the ball, but the Postman returns it with an underspin. He's totally cool, on stage, a jazzman with a saxophone, playing a song that is trying to annihilate itself. He is a monk inside a cloister in the fourteenth century, copying scrolls to keep the words from disappearing. It's a philosophy he doesn't understand, and he feels naked, trapped. In his confusion, he smashes the ball. But in order to win, he needs to work on steadiness.

In my fantasy, you do this just for me. We are in a club in Paris, late at night. I am Anais and you are Henry Miller. I am wearing a red feather boa. You are wearing a red baseball cap and red shorts. In a jeweled mirror, I watch your back ripple.

I am a hummingbird, in love, hovering over your shoulder. I am the spinning orbit of a philosophy made of bird feathers. All of the men I have ever loved are spinning inside me, in constant pursuit of perfection, some greater excellence unfolding, the artist, the body celebrating, the mind body gap closing, rendering the imaginary art, the perfect shot, the perfect universe, making it real.

The Postman is peddling up the cliffs of a small island off the coast of Italy. He is in exile on a one-speed bicycle. The tennis ball is a dancer who falls sideways into his arms.

Finding You

I dreamed of you in the desert
and in secret tunnels
below the pyramids of Giza.

In initiation chambers
you anointed my feet with jasmine oil
before my journey into the unknown.

You followed me
into the secret passageways
between lives
behind a long row of camels
where I was waiting
for the solstice sun.

I have loved you
inside wide fields of sunflowers,
in the desert with Jupiter rising
over the Eastern mountains,
Cassiopeia floating below
the midheaven,
your hands
light inside a waterfall.

Come to the place where
you can hear the ocean
through the open
skylight.

Carry the moon.
Bring your hands of silver.

If you were here,
we'd be touching.

Swan Light

Dancing in Paradise Café

I'm on the floor
with my foot extended to Cassiopeia,
toe pointing to the Pole Star.
I'm twirling into the birth
of a new galaxy,
swirling gasses condensing into the shape
of the choreography of your
left arm
as you pull me into
the salty water of a lunar sea,
where life, against all odds,
is finding its first form.

I dance in a dinosaur's dream,
the edge of a bone,
the heartbeat of a feather
finding the species and genus
of a bird that will fly
into the dance of fingers
exploring the shape of a star
at the apogee
of a dream inside an egg
etched with the wisdom
of an exploding universe.

It's the chanting of an ocean
as it discovers the shape
of a heartbeat
and remembers how to dance,
smoke inside the
breath of the buffalo
running across a primal plain
of first light,
writing on the wall of the cave

where the ocean echoes
into the curve of the penumbra
of a seashell moon.

As you dip me into the Milky Way,
my back is arcing
into the flute's high descant,
singing the memory of the future
where the secret of species is revealed
in the chord of the whir of grasshoppers
on a blue and emerald jewel
in the shape of a double helix,
remembering white fire
in the belt of Orion,
an arrow through time
dreaming the beauty of the Pleiades,
the temple dancer,
her silver bells, her back
a sequence of vectors
across oceans, across time.

By a Farmhouse in Corvallis

His hand is like a hummingbird
difficult to see or freeze frame
at each end of a wide vibrato.

Music floating
through a wind tunnel.

We kiss in a hot spring
love each other under the open sky
in shoulder high water,
his eyes radiant as the wings
of a blue heron.

We swim inside
swan light, sky ballet
lifting through the aurora.

Eggshell blue notes, crazy happy,
stolen time.

Ring of Fire

At the edge of the continent,
fires are everywhere.
Lightning strike at Point Arena,
then a wide band of fire
traveling northeast on a summer wind.
Hundreds of lightning strikes
inside a ring of fire
torching the solstice night.

In the Mendocino Woodlands,
echoes of stellar jays,
a family of pheasants,
a mountain lion stalking in the meadow.
In the distance, burning mountains.
Images of the enigma
weaving themselves together
inside a larger vision.

For some reason I don't understand,
my mother decided to walk
back from the edge –
unable to leap at this time
through the ring of fire.

This is for my mother,
the older version of the three-year-old
who stood on the piano bench
and belted out radio tunes
and folk songs from the old country
when her relatives said in Yiddish,
Sing Mamale, Sing Little Mama.

Somewhere
in the middle of the continent

peonies in full bloom
now filling the still warm nights
with their sticky fragrance.

Somewhere
while the rest of us are
still dreaming,
a meeting with her Guardian Angels,
planning how long she will stay
and the next adventure on her soul's journey.

Mamale,
you'll probably burn a path of fire
through the sky on your way,
and wherever the meteorites and snow angels
take you next,
I hope it is glorious!

In the middle of the redwood forest,
I feel you singing
inside the spirit of the trees.

Pool

My words ripple through water.
When they touch you,
you don't understand.
They escape your fingers.

Words surrounded by stones.

Words
        under
                water.

They swim inside themselves
to find their own light.

In the pool I inhale your skin.
I swim in the scent of you.
My words don't touch you
the way our kisses do.

Our toes touch as
fantail koi brush your skin
in a Japanese temple garden.

My words
swim through the water
push through
the alphabet of your skin.

Redwoods in the Early Morning

after the eclipse sings

after the crab nebula spins a supernova in my heart
after the memories
after the brilliant starry sky
constellations whispering like runes in a cryptic language

after one day maybe next week
after ice storms wrapping trees
after the stairs lead to blessings as well as sorrow

after the cellos harmonize to the prayer you used to sing
after the floating music of the waves
after the only conversation is to enjoy your own happiness

after your parents float through the tangible horizon
and their spirits have become part of you

because our lives are essentially a mystery –
redwoods floating in early morning fog,
and I have never been good with goodbyes

after the night kept getting foggier and foggier
and she flew through the corona of a distant sun

after she appeared in a lucid dream
singing the old folk melodies
as fires burned redwood trees,
releasing their seeds for the next generation.

Swan Dream

You play piano,
run through shoulder high
fields of summer corn,
disappear inside a wind tunnel.

Sunlight sprays across the room
in feathers of light.

Trills, the silver wings
of a calliope hummingbird
suddenly emerge
in a green rush of feathers
from a hidden place.

It is morning or evening,
a soft pink light
lifting through an expanding sky,
a dance of milky feathers,
a swan swimming through
a streak of rippled water.

Sunlight
makes the walls transparent,
and the sounds of the world
start rushing in.

Iowa Omen

Three hawks fly south
    as your voice trembles
        across the great plains.

Fields of sleeping cows
    a gentleness in the land.

Here is the omen:
    Sky splashed with aurora,
        blue stars, curtains of light.

The letters are gold
    on red silk –
        Japanese calligraphy.

If I had the right kind of ink
    I'd write them
        on your skin.

Circle of Stones

In the ICU, while he was dreaming
in that space-time portal between the worlds,
he must have heard the chanting
and felt deep notes resonating from the cello.
When we sang to him and played the First Bach Prelude,
I know it made him happy in his soul.

Then a single note
where the wind whispers,
he's not in this world anymore.

But the earth remembers
the red farmhouse surrounded by sunflowers,
the one lane road through the oaks,
the pond and the early green
of the earth in springtime.

Memories unfurl like a calla lily,
and it all comes back to him –
wisdom retrieved from papyrus
burned in the Alexandrian fire,
the way things done in the dark
show up in the light again.

I am singing inside a
circle of stones in the breaking dawn
at the edge of a tsunami.
Images of the Dead Sea, otherworldly.
An arc of candles leading to a star,
a child king in an Egyptian tomb.

I go to the river to swim
and rinse death
out of my black skirt.

He understands the separation between the worlds,
hard questions, difficult choices, what the soul knows.
A red rose waiting on brick stairs,
sunlight shining through red petals,
almost otherworldly.

I wish you peaceful dreams tonight –
blue stones, high cliffs, salt seas,
the caves at *Rosh Hanikra*
where the sky echoes.

You are the blessing
and you are the blessed.

Dawn after the Art Walk

Line of a train on the north side of town
an hour before sunrise.
I open the early morning window
to snow under a street lamp.
In my bedroom, a chill in the walls,
a loneliness deeper than my bones.

Changing my shoes after the last waltz,
I walk into the cold air alone.
By the door to the Landmark Hotel
at exactly the wrong moment,
I witness a marriage unraveling.
In one evening, in front of me
all of the reasons I left this place.

Dreams tumble like the paintings I saw –
tree frogs splotching a red barn
under an arch of cottonwood branches,
a dancer climbing blue star stairs
to the Pleiades.

Five years ago, I packed up
what was most important to me
in my Toyota and drove
west across the mountains.
In the back seat,
my cello, my dance shoes, my favorite books
including the one I was writing.

Somewhere inside, beyond the snow
I knew about you
and knew you were not here.

Stripes of Light on their Bodies

Through Venetian blinds
stripes of light
on an arm, a leg, an echo
a lithe twisting of bodies
shining in the half
moonlight.

At one o'clock in the morning,
a light rain in Kentucky,
a motorcycle
blasting through the echo
of an open window
under emerging branches
of a catalpa tree.

Inside the window
illumination
of intertwining fingers
a twisting, a lifting, a dance
under papaya
stripes of moonlight,
a memory of a swan
charcoal pencil tracing
the tenderness of a shoulder
the soft touch of your
fingertips.

Meditation on the Muni

When you can't understand the language,
the syllables sound like birds –
old Chinese women chirping like catbirds
perched on a mulberry branch,
searching for fermented cherries.
Norwegian, a dogsled
weaving down the mountain.
Swedish, a wobbling luge.
German and Hebrew, an argument
into the wounds of the previous century.
Nepali, rocks in a river
singing under white water.
Hindi, an amber flow of chanting honey.
French, a casual flirtation
at the painted tables of a café
by the Left Bank.
Tagalog, papayas from the Philippines.
Spanish, the music of the earth.

That man with the tattooed bull's eye
on his right leg,
a target for poison darts
blown by aboriginal tribes in the rain forest
close to the Anaconda River
or water sports in the Castro District?
The woman with blue hair
having an argument with her lover
and everyone riding the streetcar . . .
Cell phone citation?
Too loud and way too private.
No, we don't want to know.
Second citation for leopard dress clashing
with zebra boots.

I was hoping to close my eyes
and swirl into the rushing waters
of a Himalayan River,
a turquoise Ferris wheel, the dogsled
of meditation,
constellations swirling a Devanagari riddle,
then get lost in the leopard light
of an afternoon dream
or the next chapter of a Mexican novel
in the genre of magical realism –
the one with the whole town eating
animal crackers laced with a secret
potion giving everyone erotic dreams.
What was I thinking?

Butterflies

In Ms. Matsumoto's home living class,
we learned how to sit with our legs crossed.
Three times a week,
during fifth period at middle school,
we learned her version of ladylike manners.
On her clutch of neatly arranged
Japanese sofas and chairs,
we learned to converse like geishas.
We prepared and served small trays of *hors d'oeuvres* –
crackers with cheese and pickles arranged in a trident,
and learned to eat them slowly.
Under her tutelage, I developed a lifelong
love of the Triscuit.

We constructed gingham aprons
and were forced to baste every stitch,
even though I already knew how to use
the Singer sewing machine at home.
Everything took twice as long as my attention span,
and I didn't learn how to sew anything I would wear
until I brought a pattern to Grandma Helen's farm
for a circle skirt made of cotton
printed with pictures of musical instruments.

We were all butterflies
circling the halls of our education,
but I am convinced that no one learns manners
until their shining star
has circled around the sun many times.
A girl in seventh grade does not know
how her actions knock against the world
and ricochet into the fractal
of human feelings. Or how a joyful word
can make a stranger smile for the next ten years.

We wore fishnet stockings, red sandals and miniskirts.
A girl in seventh grade does not know
the power of her heartbreaking beauty.

Late August

Late August in the garden,
a final bloom of lilies
composting an echo, an angel, a dream.

Tangerine sunset over the Pacific.
My tomatoes are still laughing at me
for trying to make them grow in the coastal fog.

My stepmother has forgotten my name,
but I hope she is still dreaming of my father
waiting for her with an embrace
of starlight.

Meteor showers fall over the mountains.
After the dance tonight
ephemeral flash of light across the sky –
tiny burning.

My grandmothers stare at me
through an open window,
Andrew Wyeth curtain blowing out to the stars
as if the ancestors wait to extend their hands
and pull her up to the spirit world.

Fold the sorrow like a flag
and give it to the sun to burn.

Requiem

For Edie

The door opens on Tuesday.
On Friday she walks away from the world.
I saw them at the Symphony,
Brahms and one hundred voices around them.
He was wearing a black suit with a top hat,
she in a long silk evening gown,
his arm softly around her shoulder.
They waved at me from a high window
and then they walked into the stars.

Nobody else could see them
but they waved at me
from a high box in the air.
In the fortissimo,
low pedal tones of the organ
vibrated the ceiling and the walls,
and in the quiet moments
one hundred voices hummed
the chord of the earth
as it turned.

In another world,
she is skating on a river
in the rose pink of sunset or dawn.
A fox fur hat around her face
keeps her warm, sheltering her
as a cottonwood tree from thunder.
These memories comfort as a soft pillow,
green and cool, a meadow
glowing with wild irises and daffodils,
the path through the forest where you walked,
where the leaves of your life
glow like rhapsodies at your feet.

Coda to a Transformation

Time has become a stranger
walking barefoot into the light.
You think about sunlight through a forest
of redwood trees, a diamond under the weight
of a hidden river, the thousand ways
your life becomes your face.

After seven seasons,
your parents become your memory,
a legacy of ghosts.
They give you an ankh
and a torch to hold.
Blue flame. Mysterious music.
A tamboura from the afterlife.
Your face becomes your memory,
fiercely loving.

You're still trying to remember
the message that flashed and disappeared
from the chalkboard. A blue feather.
A copper penny on the pavement.
A window where a face
appeared and disappeared.

What was that singing from the other world?
Voices in the morning
as you gather mint and arugula
from your garden by the ocean. Salty air.
You're trying to reinvent yourself.
The feathers tell you
the message will not appear again
in the same way,
but you need to remember.

You're riding a bicycle
to a memory in Washington Heights,
the street curving up to a
total eclipse of the moon.
In a dream, the hymn of a nightingale,
the birth of a galaxy
flying out of a sea of first light.
You meet yourself in the middle
of opposite directions.

You're wanting to be brilliant
as you walk into the rain,
but further inside the supernova
of your own blossoming heart,
a deeper vision is whispering,
letting you throw
whatever stops you from dancing
into the fire.

Canon for Bears and Ponderosa Pines

Dreams of the Ecliptic

To change a girl into a kite,
    tell her that love is the moon.

To teach a tree to sing,
    put a harp under its branches.

To change a bowl of dust into a planet,
    paint watercolor rings around the ecliptic.

To change the sky into a dream,
    put a song into a hammock.

To melt an ice cube,
    light a fire under the map of the constellations.

To write a symphony in a major key,
    plant a rainbow under an apple tree.

To create a universe,
    ride on a meteor shower
        as the archer shoots a path of light
        across the sky.

When the sun rises for the first time,
    fill the sky with your singing.

Margalit

For Margalit Oved, Yemenite dancer and choreographer

"The duende surges up from the soles of the feet... It is not a matter of ability but of real, live form; of blood; of ancient culture."
- Federico Garcia Lorca, "Theory and Function of the Duende"

The younger dancer didn't have what she did –
the swaying of eucalyptus leaves in her fingers,
the taste of old world salt on her breath.
Margalit was like the flamenco dancer
with fire in her throat,
hibiscus on her lips,
belly swaying in the rhythm of the sea.

Yes, I know . . .
The violist who stopped performing
before the arc of his vibrato
passed its prime. The French horn player
who eased himself out of the opera
while his lips still had the ability to kiss his wife.
The ballerina who set up a dance academy
after her swan song.

Margalit said her protege
could execute subtle moves that her aging body
did not have the agility to perform,
but this is what I saw –
a young tree with hollow branches,
the flaming red and burnt umber
of the change of season
absent from her palette of painting oils.
Her movements lithe but lacking *duende*,
too much sunshine in her hands.

I wanted to feel
the spice of black olives in a Yemenite market,
the cucumbers and tomatoes,

the drum made from the recycled tin
that was filled with olive oil.
I wanted to feel the rhythm
of long boats pulling fish from the Mediterranean sea,
the nets of the fishermen.
I wanted to watch her veined and beautiful hands
gathering rosebuds from her mother's garden,
brass bells dreaming on her ankles
with the memory of the land where she was born,
and the way her mother carried her across the desert
to the Promised Land.

Magnificat

For J.S. Bach

It was the old man's 285th birthday –
and I mean the Maestro,
the illuminata, Johann Sebastian Bach.
I was a university student, and to celebrate
three centuries of musical genius,
our conductor led a twenty hour marathon concert
starting early in the morning.
All day, musicians and students migrated
in and out of the auditorium,
with motets, cantatas and concertos.
A bare-footed organist
played the Toccata and Fugue in D Minor,
then a prelude entirely with his feet.
I was amazed at the synergy of dance and sound.

Our concertmaster dazzled us by playing
the Sixth Bach Cello Suite, arranged for violin,
with his eyes closed. No music stand
as he tuned to an inner singing.
Segue to the entire orchestra walking on stage
to play the Second Brandenburg Concerto,
the Concerto for Two Harpsichords,
the Concerto for Three Harpsichords,
and later, just after sunset, the Magnificat.
I was playing cello next to the harpsichord,
inside the sway of its musical body,
surrounded by tones that took me back
to an earlier century.

That night, I had my first experience
of musical transcendence.
The moon was glowing through stained glass.
On the stage, we were playing the Magnificat.
Inside, we were flying in other-worldly ecstasy.

By 10:00 that night, I could swear the Maestro was there,
listening and sometimes playing with us.
Years later, on the other side of the continent,
one of my private pleasures is playing the Bach Cello Suites
late at night, with no one listening.
And sometimes, by the ocean
with the moon glowing toward full,
the old man whispers to me.

Ultra-Body over the Mountain

So Larry says to the impromptu dancer, this one is in eleven. I'd like to see what you do with it. He's playing silver flute with a trio of jazz musicians at Union Square, high notes fluttering through a curtain of butterflies, musical nectar flying from the piano and fretless bass. She has already taken over the open space in front of the stage, smiling coyly like a geisha, winking behind her paper umbrella.

The dancer spins out of a time warp, waving peacock feathers. Black slinky pants gyrating like a snake. So thin she does not need her pink leopard bra, so she tosses it to the audience. She whirls like a dervish, a helicopter, a typhoon, her long black hair flying under a straw hat edged with a brown ribbon. The ribbon, the edge of a solar system. Her turquoise glass bead earrings orbiting like planets on a belly dancer's belt. Arc of sun shining on silver, spraying light.

Piano, flute and bass begin riffing "Ultra-Body over the Mountain." Larry's tune. The dancer, maybe Japanese, way over the hill. Arms flying, leg kicked over her shoulder. She's a unicorn leaping through time. After the rippling cadences of the flute solo, she knows the applause are for her. She opens her arms to the crowd, blows kisses to the audience.

A homeless man in bright green shorts orbits the square, sweetly happy for these few moments. His hands remember the trumpet he used to play, his childhood friend's conga drum. The bass improvisation is floating into an African dance, tribal rhythms swaying his legs and back. He leaves the lunch someone gave him on the stage. He has to keep dancing. No roof over his memories, an ocean of sky, floating with boat-shaped clouds.

A circular wind from the ocean is spinning across the stage. The Japanese dancer has become a unicorn. She almost smiles. A shower of glass beads whirls around her, the planets of a tiny universe, with meteor showers burning a path through the stars. Her stars.

The unicorn spins through time, her long Japanese hair flying in the wind. Almost a pirouette, as much as the concrete will allow. Over the mountain, maybe a moon, maybe a sun. Perhaps a butterfly. The tune climbs the mountain – weaving and winding to its slinky final chord. The butterfly bows, deep diva, face to the floor, arms flying to the moon, to the moon, to the moon.

Cello Lesson

Down a flight of stairs
on a snowy evening
in Ashland by Lithia Park.
He's playing Bach
in the cheese shop
as diners finish their brie,
flatbread, soup and wine,
some listening, some not.

We sit on a stone bench,
for this moment
forgetting to order tea
or an oatmeal cookie.
We're here for the music
and when he plays the D-Minor
Bach Sarabande
by memory, with his eyes closed,
it opens my heart.

Later, he flies into my dream,
a yellow bird
singing high rippling notes
I can't follow with my cello.

As the full moon shimmers the ocean,
I hear him whisper . . .

Let all technique
fly out the window
into the salty waves
and from your heart
let that beautiful note
fly.

Emotions expand into vibrato,
color and light,
a curtain of blue butterflies.
The first note of the Popper Requiem,
a meteorite
falling into the ocean.

And that perfect note
I so desperately want
and can almost feel in my body,
swimming so deep
inside me . . .

It's something about the heart
breaking open.

Under a Copper Moon

After the storm, a dream buffalo
nested in our yard
surrounded by lavender.

Buffalo clouds
thundering on the horizon.
Clouds like white turtles
crawling across a wide lake of sky,
blue and shimmering.

When a buffalo enters your dream,
listen for arpeggio hooves,
the weight of music,
a copper moon
above a vanishing prairie.

Timpani of thunder pounding red clay,
the weight of time.
The light at the edge of the universe.

Canon for Bears and Ponderosa Pines

Maybe a canon, like bears climbing a mountain,
the impossible note, the way a string vibrates
at the intersection of bow and memory.
A calliope hummingbird
hovering over a branch of hibiscus
before the green wings lift, dive, flit
into the invisible.

The impossible climb, the arpeggio
of a sacred mountain in Nepal
where they don't allow human trekkers.
The color of sky, a single line of pink over silver,
ethereal, flooded with light
before the sun falls into the Dudh Kosi River.

Sometimes, music feels impossible,
something buried so deep inside me
it could take a lifetime
for my fingers to learn
the cello's toning to what I hear.
A canon for bears and ponderosa pines,
a garden of calla lilies unfurling,
a night of peonies, tiny ants
opening trills of blooms.

Impossible, but I try it anyway,
the sun blinding, climbing the Himalayas
over the icefall, the shadow of Dhaulagiri
tumbling down the river, a cascade of minor notes
so sweet, a mountain bird drunk with song,
a snow leopard disappearing behind an avalanche.
The roaring pulls you out of your tent,
out of a dream, into the night
where the music, like a snow leopard,
is impossible.

Years ago, I dreamed a four part canon
all night, the voices like honey,
bears climbing a mountain
lit with early morning sun, the ponderosa pines
singing notes on a pipe organ
in a cathedral of trees,
sunlight pouring through the colors
and shape of a high window.

All of the trees in the forest
sang to me that night,
the canon weaving a gentle wind
through the branches. I will never forget the joy
I felt that morning, sun filtering
into a pentagonal room, stained glass windows,
the ocean humming in the distance.

Sometimes, remembering
is a feeling without a form,
the bears scattered into the forest,
their footprints changing shape,
climbing a mountain of melting snow.
Sometimes, the ponderosa pines whisper, like love
like music. The memory
beyond my fingers.

It is the poem that cannot be written,
the memory of beauty,
the canon, amber light in a cathedral,
the moon rising over a forest of ponderosa pines,
black bears lost in their winter dreams,
the memory of a trout
leaping over white water,

the river singing, the music, suddenly
at the edge of possible.

Joy, like a Purple Balloon

For Erik

That morning, a man and his young daughter
were crossing Geary Boulevard
as we waited for the light.
They were both wearing purple
and she was holding three helium balloons
on long strings. Her tiny hands
floating with joy,
the balloons, a kaleidoscope of color.
The two of them
carrying all of the joy
of the human race.
I thought at that moment
if someone from another galaxy
wanted to visit life on this planet,
I would want it to be
right here and right now.
You told me you hoped
that tiny child
would hold tightly to the strings.
And at that moment, I thought
what a miracle, you and I,
among all the humans
on this flying jewel of a planet,
were lucky enough to find each other.
A miracle, a gift –
your heart filling with music,
my heart full with joy.
At our wedding, all around us
friends, family and joy
like a huge bouquet of purple balloons
floating, flapping, flying
in a wild wind.

Igneous

Eat this stone
from the kitchen of the earth
Toss it into the magma
of a volcano

Marinate
the boulder
Slide it into a stone pie
to be baked
in Earth's oven
Doing what it does best

Skip this stone
over a crater lake
water in the mouth
of the igneous
soup

Wear a garnet tie
a ruby ring, shale shoes
a tiara of opals
luminous with dreams

And like a child
humming a stone tune
searching for a path of pebbles
through the geckos, the dinosaurs
in a folk tale,
put it in your pocket

Walk out of the forest
where rhododendron trees
map hexagons of blossoms
under your footsteps

And let the stone
in your pocket
whisper its secrets
to the moon
to the shower of asteroids
to the singing sky

WHAT YOUR CAT DID DURING YOUR VACATION AT THE GRAND CANYON

I was walking down my very own street when Poppy, the rescue cat who lives next door, attacked a Siberian Husky. She's in the habit of attacking large dogs. Sometimes, she thinks my husband is a large dog.

Before she was rescued, her owner jumped off the Golden Gate Bridge. Full moon, facing the city as he flew.

When Beverly took her home, Poppy was afraid of everything. Now, she is sometimes friendly, but later changes her mind and hisses at tricycles and the mailman. Then she stretches, rolls, and does cat yoga on the sidewalk. Poppy likes to swat butterflies and eat basil leaves from my garden. She is random in her fickleness.

Beverly is riding a mule down a switchback in the Grand Canyon. The Bright Angel Trail. My husband unlocks the door to her duplex, and Poppy meows and purrs before she eats. She has plenty to say until her food dish hits the floor. Content at last, or at least, quiet. A few minutes later, Poppy forgets who he is and attacks him from the balcony.

I wonder what happened during those five days before they found her. And the five days before he jumped. Imaginary mice running across the balcony. Bridges and bones. Daddy howling at the moon.
At night, I wonder what she dreams.

When You Fly

Things that might be a bomb . . .
Yogurt, avocados, lemonade, iced tea
the endpin of a cello

A banjo, a violin
electronic equipment wrapped carefully
in cotton fabric and bubble wrap
so it won't be damaged after landing

The Empire State Building
The Golden Gate Bridge
The packing cases of the San Francisco Symphony
The Eiffel Tower
The Pyramids at Giza

The unwritten pages of a novel
in the genre of magical realism
An architectural drawing
An algorithm, a vector
An illuminated medieval book of hours
My grandmother's wedding ring

And to the TSA agent
who groped me during the pat down
and then asked me out to lunch . . .

It's not a hand grenade;
it's an avocado.

Earthquake, 5 A.M.

Temblor wakes me with a kiss.
On the other side of the wall,
a whirring of water.
I open thin blinds to calla lilies,
belladonna, the garden of early
morning light.

After the earthquake
the neighborhood dogs howl,
then a silence
that wraps the morning.

Jar with Dragons

A walk through the Asian Art Museum in San Francisco

1.
Jar with dragons among clouds.
Ribbons of red and green wind.
Sunflowers blooming out of nowhere
calling me back through time
to an owl, a fish, a woven knot.

2.
Notice the ripples, the sway of the river
how the sun illuminated
a carved boat
on a river without a name.
A silver vessel laden with scrolls,
papyrus inscribed with memories of
love nights under a copper moon,
what the Pharaohs dreamed.

3.
Ashes in a ceremonial urn
surrounded by fossils of shells
that were used as money,
traded for sesame oil, rice and fish.
An enamel box
where pelicans escape
behind centuries of hand-rolled glass.

4.
Bottle with melon-shaped body
and the legs of an elephant.
Bowl with peony and lotus,
orbiting the memory
of a honey-scented wind.
Moonlight scattered through branches
over the koi pond.

A world remembered in porcelain,
topaz blue and ancient light.

5.
Notice the way the dragon appears
out of nowhere.
The girl who will be a geisha
riding the tortoise,
her wings still attached, but transparent.
The lacquered box she holds,
inlaid with mother of pearl,
a secret you are not allowed to enter.

6.
What captured me was simple.
A turquoise sky above the peonies.
Tiny boats like lanterns
floating around an island
of red maple trees.
Full moon above a floating world.

7.
The wood becomes a river,
a galaxy, an eye.
A story told slowly,
through centuries.
By the ocean, the full moon
ripples the water,
Venus and Jupiter still hovering
above the horizon.
The music comes from inside,
but after carving
the wood remembers how to sing.

Six Months in Arosa

The photographs are gone,
but I still remember birds flying to my hand,
squirrels eating hazelnuts from my fingers,
and Sunday morning bells that echoed through the valley.
The Alpine houses in Switzerland had gardens of wildflowers,
and they told us the milk was so sweet
because the cows ate flowers.

On Thursdays, we hiked further up the mountain
to a tiny church in a pasture,
or sometimes down to the village
for chocolate.
An old man swept the hiking paths
with a straw broom,
and the nuns taught us the few words we knew
of Swiss German.

We were high enough in the Alps
that it snowed twice that summer.
I was learning to be a meditation teacher,
and our guru descended from a helicopter
every few weeks
to bless us and answer questions.

Every morning, fresh bread and sweet butter
on the table. Long meditations
and early morning, as dawn was breaking
and the mountains began to sing,
visions of other worlds revealed themselves.

In October, after the snow came for real,
I took the train to Chur,
speeding down the mountain
through an amazement of branches
and snow. I knit a scarf

that wrapped around my head three times,
and rainbowed to my knees.

As I was hiking, the moonstone I wore every day
fell into the snow
along with a tiny lacquered photograph of my guru,
maybe an omen
of a very independent soul.
But something deep and silent
extended like moonlight through the mountain,
and wove through my heart and mind,
my dreams and my bones. My memories,
a thousand cows clanging their bells
in the early morning.

Best Day Ever

By the Cherry Blossom Sushi Bar,
the sky is full of Japanese kites
fluttering like koi
in the ocean-scented San Francisco wind.
A girl runs down the street
laughing with her father. She's eating
a mango ice cream cone
and wearing a purple sequin sweatshirt
with a message: Best Day Ever!

I think of my father
in a parallel, interpenetrating world.
He loved sashimi
and would have wanted to come with me
today, for lunch and conversation.
I would tell him about playing
Beethoven's Ninth Symphony
on the same stand as my husband.
We'd talk about my new novel, narrated by a mermaid,
and finally weeks of open time
to call it into being.
Best Day Ever!

Six years ago in the morning,
my father left this world.
Over time, his memory
became a source of strength to me,
and joy. I would have wanted him
to give me away at our wedding,
but maybe he was doing that
in a parallel, interpenetrating world.
Best Day Ever!

I am left only with today,
another morning of light, a gift

to be in this world, drinking green tea,
watching the street parade
through floor to ceiling windows,
then indulging my mile a day walking habit
at the beach, before the wind
picks up from the Pacific.
Tonight, a Solstice Dance. I will wear
velvet, sparkles and lace
when StringFire plays a waltz
called "Solstice Wedding."

City of the Past, City of the Future.
Sunlight filled with joy.
A homeless man by the Symphony
asks if I have brought him a tangerine today.
Yes, three of them, some toothpaste, a fig bar
and a new pair of socks.
I wonder if my father sees me today
or if he is far away.
I wonder what he has learned
in the City of Immortality
and how it will feel to meet him there one day.

Back on Planet Earth,
I walk to the Post Office,
the thrift store, the bagel shop,
the fruit and vegetable stand.
And from that other world
I hear him whisper,
You were born to live in the City of Joy.
Every day, choose to walk there.
Back at home, rainbow over the ocean,
unexpected light.
Best Day Ever!

Books by Diane Frank

While Listening to the Enigma Variations: New and Selected Poems

Fog and Light: San Francisco through the Eyes of the Poets Who Live Here

Letters from a Sacred Mountain Place: A Journey through the Nepal Himalayas

Canon for Bears and Ponderosa Pines

Yoga of the Impossible

Blackberries in the Dream House

River of Earth and Sky: Poems for the Twenty-First Century

Swan Light

Entering the Word Temple

The Winter Life of Shooting Stars

The All Night Yemenite Café

Rhododendron Shedding Its Skin

Isis: Poems by Diane Frank

About the Author

Diane Frank is author of eight books of poems, three novels, and a photo memoir of her 400 mile trek in the Himalayas. Her friends describe her as a harem of seven women in one very small body. She lives in the San Francisco Bay Area, where she dances, plays cello, and creates her life as an art form. Diane teaches at San Francisco State University and Dominican University. She plays cello in the Golden Gate Symphony. *Blackberries in the Dream House*, her first novel, won the Chelson Award for Fiction and was nominated for the Pulitzer Prize. *Canon for Bears and Ponderosa Pines* received honors in the San Francisco Book Festival.

To schedule readings, book signings and workshops, and to invite her to speak to your book club, contact:

E-mail: GeishaPoet@aol.com
Website: www.dianefrank.net

Glass Lyre Press

exceptional works to replenish the spirit

Glass Lyre Press is an independent literary publisher interested in technically accomplished, stylistically distinct, and original work. Glass Lyre seeks diverse writers that possess a dynamic aesthetic and an ability to emotionally and intellectually engage a wide audience of readers.

Glass Lyre's vision is to connect the world through language and art. We hope to expand the scope of poetry and short fiction for the general reader through exceptionally well-written books, which evoke emotion, provide insight, and resonate with the human spirit.

Poetry Collections
Poetry Chapbooks
Select Short & Flash Fiction
Anthologies

www.GlassLyrePress.com

www.ingramcontent.com/pod-product-compliance
Lightning Source LLC
Chambersburg PA
CBHW030321100526
44592CB00010B/520